THE
BOLD
ONES

**INNOVATE AND DISRUPT
TO BECOME TRULY INDISPENSABLE**

SHAWN KANUNGO

NEW YORK CHICAGO SAN FRANCISCO ATHENS LONDON MADRID
MEXICO CITY MILAN NEW DELHI SINGAPORE SYDNEY TORONTO

1 2 3 4 5 6 7 8 9   LCR   27 26 25 24 23 22

ISBN   978-1-264-66915-8
MHID   1-264-66915-1

e-ISBN   978-1-264-66961-5
e-MHID   1-264-66961-5

Library of Congress Cataloging-in-Publication Data
Names: Kanungo, Shawn, author.
Title: The bold ones : innovate and disrupt to become truly indispensable / Shawn Kanungo.
Description: New York : McGraw Hill, [2023] | Includes bibliographical references and index.
Identifiers: LCCN 2022038339 (print) | LCCN 2022038340 (ebook) | ISBN ISBN 9781264669158 (hardback) | ISBN 9781264669615 (ebook)
Subjects: LCSH: Interruption (Psychology) | Technological innovations. | Career development. | Personality.
Classification: LCC BF378.I65 K46 2023 (print) | LCC BF378.I65 (ebook) | DDC 158—dc23/eng/20220914
LC record available at https://lccn.loc.gov/2022038339
LC ebook record available at https://lccn.loc.gov/2022038340

CONTENTS

CONTENTS

CHAPTER 1

THE DNA OF
THE BOLD ONES

In 1991, Sony announced a partnership with Nintendo. The two companies agreed to create a world-changing video game masterpiece, combining both their areas of expertise into one, powerhouse, Japanese-engineered console.

For Sony, this was a timid step into a new venture. Previously, the company had looked down on video gaming as a notch beneath its highbrow electronics company. To the staunch businessmen running the top of Sony, video games were simply "toys, so why on earth would they join the toy business?"[1]

But after much negotiation with Nintendo, and after consulting with a bold man who happened to work for both of them—Ken Kutaragi—they'd been talked into it. They would dive into the business of child playthings. And they were going to do it with the number one video game company in the world, Nintendo. Sony announced the partnership at the Consumer Electronics Show in Chicago on May 28, 1991.[2]

That was Tuesday.

On Wednesday, everything changed.

Nintendo had other plans. It reversed course without warning. It was ditching its agreement, and Sony, altogether. Instead, it was going to go with one of Sony's foreign competitors—the Dutch company, Philips. It's no wonder that many speculate Sony's next move was purely out of revenge.

Kutaragi, the individual who'd been partially responsible for pushing for the partnership, was working for Sony but moonlighting for Nintendo simultaneously. He stood up in a Sony meeting that was designed to kill off the video game console idea entirely. He looked directly at Sony's CEO, Norio Ohga, and he asked the one question that changed video game history:

Are you going to sit back
and accept what Nintendo did to us?

Game on.

Sony started the PS/X project, and the result was the first CD-ROM–based game console, the PlayStation. The second version, the PlayStation 2, would go on to sell over 155 million consoles, becoming the most popular game console ever created.[3]

Kutaragi's question sparked a Japanese business war—and changed the history of video gaming.

Kutaragi was in the right place at the right time, but his attendance was built on decades of tinkering, of hammering away with an engineering mind.

Far away from the hotbed of Japanese electronics, he'd been interested in engineering and mechanics since childhood, taking apart various mechanisms in his house, no doubt to the chagrin of his parents.

After college, he chose Sony because he saw it as the most "creative." When the Nintendo Entertainment System came out, he did what he'd always done since childhood; he took it apart, piece by piece, asking himself, *How can I improve this?*

His interest in electronics—along with his drive for innovation—would become a cornerstone throughout his career.

Legend has it that Kutaragi stayed up at all hours of the night to finish the first Sony PlayStation. In fact, he'd supposedly been working on it *before* Sony gave him the green light. He just couldn't help himself.

Kutaragi's interest kept pushing him to tinker. His courage kept enabling him to challenge the status quo: He did a side job for Nintendo, *while* employed at Sony, a move that almost got him fired. Later he challenged the executives at Sony to enter the video game space; many told him that "it's a terrible idea." And later he pushed Sony to broker a deal with Nintendo to enter into a new space. When that fell through, he told Sony to go it alone.

Kutaragi's idea kept him up at night, working in his basement. Then his willingness to speak against the status quo allowed him to partner with exactly the company he needed to develop what would become the world's greatest video game console.

What if that young engineer, Kutaragi, hadn't been willing to pursue his passion projects? Then what if he hadn't had the boldness to challenge the status quo thinking of his bosses at Sony?

THE BOLD ONES

The PlayStation's dominance sounds like the epitome of a timeless tale—an innovative upstart has an idea, and maybe some technical chops. Frequently such people overcome organizational obstacles, conquer their own failures, and even rise above their socioeconomic status. The reward of their perseverance is often total upheaval of a company, an industry, or even a country—in a word, they *disrupt*.

We can glance around and find these innovators everywhere.

In politics, there's Margaret Thatcher, who stepped into a world of men, took on a country in economic recession, and challenged a mentality trending toward softness. She danced on their sexism and overthrew their agendas. In sports, there's Steph Curry, whose three-point style upended everything incumbents thought they knew about basketball. In video entertainment, there's Mr. Beast, who invested millions of dollars into each of his YouTube videos and catapulted himself into fame. The military has Julius Caesar and Kublai Khan. The arts has Andy Warhol and Frida Kahlo. History discusses Rosa Parks, Galileo, and Cleopatra.

In every time period, every industry, every corner of our society, disruptors have tinkered, have destroyed, and have risen. You can hate them, love them, vilify them, or idolize them. But you can't write a history book without them.

Gone or still with us, playboys or scientists, engineers or consultants, day workers or doctors, influencers or artists, lawyers or software developers, they all have some things in common:

For one, they're unafraid.

They challenge incumbents, dismiss traditional thinking, and reinvent themselves. No matter where they go, whether into an office, a prison cell, or their own enterprise, they change everything.

I call them Bold Ones.

Bold Ones are those who are brave enough to fundamentally reinvent themselves, challenge norms, and revolutionize their worlds. Bold Ones think, act, and build for a future they see, one that others close their eyes to. They form their own understanding, confront ingrained ideas, innovate toward the future, and evolve in their careers.

Not only are these Bold Ones ready for change, but they actively anticipate it, adapt as necessary, and even *create* change themselves. They take advantage of new technologies, marketplace crashes, geographical changes, and political opportunities to disrupt their own fields and cement lasting legacies.

And here's the kicker: The Bold Ones of the past left us all the breadcrumbs, ideas in the dark, secrets on the wall. Buried within their sometimes seemingly erratic or random successes, they gave us all a map to our own disruptive future.

In this book, I want to expose you to those secrets, those breadcrumbs, through stories, experiences, ideas, tactics, and strategies, so you can innovate on your own, right where you are, and begin to flex your disruptive muscles.

THE ERA OF THE ONES

Disruption is a common topic in modern professional circles. From finance to software to healthcare to consumer packaged goods, we've all heard the stories of Blockbuster, Kodak, and Netflix. Every time, the story reads like a script: "Once-successful incumbent moves slow; fast-moving upstart defeats incumbent." There's no lesson conveyed, no depth of imagination.

The deeper story—the "disruption conversation"—feels reserved for the few established leaders who run empires and protect institutions. In this way, the message portrayed is only "thought leaders" can show other "thought leaders" how to *protect* traditionalism from Bold Ones, defend against disruption, and overcome the fallout.

That script is tired, the narrator is missing the point, and the audience is all wrong.

I want to (finally) flip the script, uncover the truth, and speak to a new breed of people. Because the truth is there, lurking—there are lessons to be learned, ideas to be copied, and processes to be replicated. Don't worry; we'll get to all that.

But first, let me say this about the audience: It's time for a reorientation. Let's change who we're talking to about disruption.

Let's start the conversation by talking directly to the individuals—you and me—who can truly create tomorrow's industries.

Every company seems to concern itself with defending against a Kutaragi upset, a new entrant like LIV Golf, a Warby Parker play, or (insert your favorite disruptive story here). But what if we changed the conversation and started *embracing* the Kutaragis of the world? In fact, what if we, the ones sitting in the offices, doing the work, feeling the changes, actually *became* the disruptors?

The next true disruption isn't going to happen in an office of traditionalism anyway, so let's bring the conversation out into the streets.

The next person who disrupts the accounting world will be a solo accountant. The next big media entity will be one person with a mic. The next game-changing venture capitalist will be a solo operator. When someone rethinks factory floor plans to create a speedier, safer, and more efficient production method, that person will have a first and last name without the suffix of "incorporated."

In his book *Never Eat Alone*, Keith Ferrazzi says it like this: "For much of the last 150 years of economic history, the smartest people gravitated to where the money was. The money, today, is looking for where the smartest people are."

No longer are individuals attaching themselves to companies; companies are attaching themselves to individuals.

Today we have an entire industry called the "creator economy," brands built around personalities that attract real people and real dollars. In 1984, when the Chicago Bulls rookie Michael Jordan signed a $500,000, five-year shoe deal with Nike, it was shocking. Rookies simply didn't get that kind of deal. Today it's a no-brainer. I advise some companies in the direct-to-consumer space, and their primary method of customer acquisition is leveraging individuals like Michael Jordan to gain market share. Not advertisements, not billboards, but individuals. Because individuals hold all the power. That's why you have YouTubers such as Logan Paul or the Nelk Boys who can create their own consumer packaged goods companies, or why solo writers like Ben Thompson are generating millions through their own blogs. It's why Udemy instructors like Rob Percival are making seven figures teaching kids how to code, and finance TikTok stars have lucrative financial planning businesses.

We are living in the Era of the Ones.

INSIDE OR OUT—YOU MUST INNOVATE

Let's clarify something from the jump: being a Bold One doesn't mean we must, or even should, all become solo flights of brave entrepreneurism. That life may be for some, but for most of us, the best path forward is to start innovating right where we are, inside our offices, within our companies. That's another reason Kutaragi's story offers such fresh insight—today when people are in a rush to start their own business, Kutaragi reminds us that innovation can happen not just in spite of, but within, an incumbency.

The resources, feedback, and collaboration that institutions provide are invaluable catalysts for disruptors. Bold Ones take advantage of these resources to accelerate their ideas and give legs to the future.

When Kutaragi pushed the PlayStation, he wasn't just saving himself, but the company he worked for. And it's a good thing he did; the PlayStation would go on to deliver *90 percent* of Sony's profits for several years.

You aren't just a small cog in the wheel of your company's future—you may be *the* solution their survival.

When you become a Bold One, you find fulfillment. You stop thinking that somewhere else will make you better. You realize that anywhere you go, *you* can make *it* better.

Inside or outside, innovators push the envelope. The point isn't where they are; it's what they have on the inside—a desperate need to upset the status quo. You may be a speechwriter wanting to bring honesty into the political spectrum, an electrician hoping to utilize modern project management processes, or a corporate buyer wanting to overhaul your distribution model.

———

Sometime around 500 BC the Greek philosopher Heraclitus said, "The only constant in life is change." The ancient world did evolve, but to modern humanity, it evolved annoyingly slowly. It took nearly two millennia before a printer was invented that could mass-produce Heraclitus's words into books. Yet from the time the printing press was invented, it only took *half* a millennium before Charles Darwin published *On the Origin of Species*, the book that defined evolutionary biology. And only a century after that, Peter Diamandis keenly added to Heraclitus's words, noting, "The only constant is change," but now "The rate of change is increasing exponentially."

Change always occurs more quickly than some are ready for, which is the definition of disruption: a change that occurs so rapidly that it displaces the unprepared. The only difference between our world and Heraclitus's is that disruption now occurs at a rate never before anticipated.

Entire industries, such as banking and software, are converging, creating new marketplaces and displacing others. Modern technologies, such as artificial intelligence and Web3, are spreading across the entire globe to the most distant corners, driving adoption in countries that don't even have access to clean water. Roles such as content creation and sales are combining to create new jobs, requiring skills that academia is struggling to understand, much less teach. Individuals with established tenure are demanding flexibility and lifestyle changes, leaving organizations at an unprecedented rate to reinvent their own careers and lifestyles.

In their individual workplace, future disruptors may be unable to articulate exactly what's happening, but they can feel it nonetheless. You may not have the words, but like the pull of an undercurrent before it's visible from the shore, you can sense that the waters are changing.

If you want to redefine an industry, or if you simply want to get your boss to listen to you about a small change, there are two keys you will need to unlock your own inner disruptor.

The first is an insatiable need to innovate.

Let's revisit Kutaragi. Well before his foray into video game technology, he'd bumped up into the firewall of the status quo. After working on an early LCD screen and a floppy disk, Kutaragi kept pushing the envelope, wanting more creative, futuristic projects. He found the edge of what his company's mindset would allow, and asked one too many questions. (Once, a coworker even told him, "You must never say that at Sony."[4])

How Kutaragi landed the side gig at Nintendo is the stuff of legend: Apparently Nintendo called Sony because Nintendo needed help with the sound engineering for the audio chip inside the Super NES. Kutaragi happened to answer the phone. He said yes to the request, and without asking for permission, he worked on the project in secret. He just couldn't help himself.

When Misty Copeland took her first ballet class, she'd missed the normal timetable to become a good, much less a great, ballerina. Plus, she didn't look like most of the others in ballet classes. But she didn't care—she kept practicing anyway, until she eventually became the first black prima ballerina in the American Ballet Theater's 75-year history.

When Volodymyr Zelensky decided it was time to change Ukraine's politics, it didn't matter that he was simply an actor who played a president on TV. He just *had* to make a move.

Bold Ones are haunted by one unstoppable thought: "I don't want to get left behind."

If you're reading this book, you probably have something inside of you—something that's screaming about innovation. You may feel intimidated or exhilarated, but you can hear the internal ghost screaming, "Innovate or die."[5]

If that's you, I know a little how you feel. That's exactly how I've felt for a long time.

MY STORY

When I began my 12-year stint at Deloitte, I started in accounting. After a couple of years, I transferred to management consulting, where I had the chance to advise leading organizations and governments.

I immediately recognized that my colleagues at Deloitte gave every single deliverable and pitch with old-school PowerPoint decks, complete with lackluster visuals and a laser pointer. *Seriously, we've been doing* this *for decades?* I thought.

I considered asking if we could update our deliverable method. But while I had great bosses who typically gave me a long leash, I could just "feel" that questioning wouldn't go over well.

So I didn't ask.

I just jumped.

Instead of the nearly templatized decks my cohorts used, I leaned on my visual chops and created film documentaries for my clients to offer a stunning visual appeal. I also used my *personal* credit card to purchase new hardware and software. I bought video equipment and a Mac. I tapped my own network to develop digital prototypes. I used crowdsourcing and freelance marketplaces to create prototypes and develop other assets. Bold? Yes. But did I get in trouble? No. Here's a secret I discovered early on about innovation:

Bosses don't say, "*I* was wrong."
They say, "*We* were right."

When you make a bold bet and others love it, bosses celebrate you and take part in the congratulations, as if the idea were their own.

Over time, employees frequently requested to join my team, and clients started coming to the firm specifically asking for me. I challenged old-school thinking wherever I found it.

At one point my team was talking about hosting a business roundtable and inviting innovative movers and shakers from across the continent. When we were discussing who the participants would be, I blurted out, "Let's get the premier."[6] My colleagues looked at me as if I were insane, but I called the premier anyway. And she agreed to come.

What next? I thought.

I cold-called Apple.

This was 2013, and Apple wanted to flex one of its latest disruptive technologies—the iPad—for the business world. Wanting to be part of the action, Apple immediately mailed a ton of its hottest iPads to be featured at the event, pro bono.

I soon built a reputation for moving fast, and not always asking permission. The firm's partners were fairly agreeable, but don't worry—I still managed to ruffle feathers a few times. Once, after a particularly bold move, one of the managing partners called me to simply say, "Just give me a heads-up next time *before* you do anything crazy."

Alongside my work at Deloitte, I continued to explore new frontiers. I teamed up with outside colleagues to launch a film production group, Nelson Spooner Productions. Although our films won just three local awards, being part of the process allowed me to fall in love with video. In 2013, I also cofounded a mobile application firm that created a couple of brief but buzz-worthy apps (Pressmoi and Roman).

At Deloitte I eventually moved into the role of senior manager within strategy, where innovation became my brand. Third-party companies started inviting me to speak at conferences across the globe on innovation and disruption strategy.

By 2018, I'd left Deloitte and dedicated my time to speaking and advising companies on disruption. But the turning point really came in 2020, at the height of the pandemic. By then I was giving close to 60 keynotes a year, but overnight, conferences were universally canceled.

My team and I seized the moment by asking a simple, bold question: "How do we create the best virtual keynote anyone has ever seen?"

Using the Myer Horowitz Theatre in Edmonton, and my understanding of videography and visual appeal, my team reinvented the look and feel of a virtual keynote. We managed to give more keynotes in 2020 than in any year prior. We did it again in 2021.

Why does it matter? As I've traveled the globe, connecting with hundreds of CEOs and frontline workers, sitting in hundreds of boardrooms, and meeting with creators at every level, here's what I can tell you:

Bold Ones are everywhere.

They're sitting in cubicles, creating spreadsheets. They're pouring steamed milk into coffee at Starbucks. They're typing away at their laptop sitting in the lobby. They're at a boardroom meeting listening to the same pitch they heard last year, knowing it's exactly what will put their company into a "has-been, once-was" category. They can feel the tides turning. If you can feel it too, let me tell you:

It's because you have what it takes to be a Bold One.

You just need permission, and a path forward.

I've been studying the world's greatest disruptors—innovators who were unafraid to challenge ideas, create new processes, and even sacrifice their own reputations to do so. They pop up everywhere, since humanity's genesis: from Joan of Arc to Hasan Minhaj, from Madame Curie to Elon Musk, from Copernicus to Lil Nas X, from Angela Merkel to Queen Elizabeth. I've learned something: They all left clues.

If we refuse to accept these examples as one-in-a-million David-and-Goliath triumphs, we can put their individual stories together to create a map, one that will lead us to individual success.

Galileo taught us to challenge incumbent thinking. Shakespeare showed how to democratize the arts. Oprah

Winfrey demonstrated how to create a voice more powerful than an incumbent media company.

In this book, I've distilled these lessons into eight main paths, trailblazed by eight of the world's unlikeliest innovators. We'll explore history's heroes and villains; we'll learn from artists and scientists, the living and the dead, businesses and athletes, intrapreneurs and entrepreneurs.

Each chapter will open by highlighting the Bold One. Then I'll guide you through how we can emulate their strategy in our own roles and society.

FROM AUBREY TO DRAKE

I've always been fascinated with individual disruptors—people that could change their industries forever. In one of my first presentations on disruption back in 2014, I dissected a rapper's rise, and I asked the audience a simple question about them: "Was he truly disruptive?"

He broke records set by the Beatles and Michael Jackson, at one point claiming 9 out of the 10 top songs in the country.[7] He beat out Rihanna and Madonna—having created 54 top-10 hits. He's performed alongside legends such as 2 Chainz, Jay-Z, and Lil Wayne, outselling artists like Tupac and Eminem.

His parents called him Aubrey Graham, but you probably know him as Drake.

Drake didn't grow up in a hip-hop haven like Los Angeles, New York City, or Dallas—he grew up in Toronto, Canada (a fellow Canadian!). He didn't even start out in music.

In 2001, his million-watt smile landed him a role on *Degrassi: The Next Generation*, where he was making a decent living, at about $40,000 a year. As it turned out, it wasn't what

Drake was doing during the day that mattered, but what he was doing under the shadows of the moonlight.

While on the phone with his imprisoned father, his dad's cellmate started rapping for Drake, who started jotting down lyrics in response. That lyrical moment ignited a fire. As *GQ* put it in 2013, "He dropped out of high school, acted all day, and rapped all night." He released *Room for Improvement* in 2006, with 23 tracks on it, while still working at *Degrassi*.

The rest is history, still in the making,

One day, he was a Canadian actor with charisma and good looks. The next, he was one of the greatest hip-hop artists of all time.

Earlier we discussed the first of two keys you need to start your own journey to innovation, to becoming a Bold One. The first one was an insatiable desire to innovate.

Now we define the second key. It's one you'll need to access again and again as you turn these pages—it's your own hidden desire, the skill you have that you aren't quite showcasing to the world, the one thing you *really* want to pursue. The wild idea that eats in your brain, "like a splinter in your mind,"[8] while you're sending in reports, attending Zoom meetings, and finalizing project documents.

Your true passion may be in the role you're currently in, or it could be in an adjacent category, or perhaps it's in something else altogether. I've met insurance brokers locked into a nine-to-five who are Googling "Ethereum" on their lunch break, lawyers who have a diehard passion for real estate, and rocket scientists who are fascinated with the beer made in distilleries.

That thing you're Googling, that quirky interest you have, isn't an accident. When you're diving into those Reddit forums or Discord servers, your innovative gene is calling out. It's a not-so-hidden desire to disrupt, and it's itching for expression. That draw to a new technology or process, or something that can't be explained just yet, is the connecting point between your uniqueness and the future. It's a convergence of today's technology, coming trends, and your unique makeup.

THE BOLD ONES

Take one more look at the names of history's Bold Ones. Remember that they're names of *people*, not companies. That matters to you and to me. We are real people, with real names, with real gifts, talents, and unique views of the marketplace based on our geographies, our experiences, our clients, and our skill sets.

You already have the DNA of a disruptor, and here's how I know: Those nights when you've stayed up late designing a business model or researching a new technology prove it. So do those times when you bite your tongue at work. Or those moments when you daydream about how a fresh idea could upend your industry. If you've felt the waters shifting, then you have something in common with a Bold One.

I want to give your internal desire the chance to express itself.

If you don't find a way to express your creativity, someone else will. You'll watch as the marketplace changes and leaves you behind. You'll never execute on that genius plan you had. You'll never speak to your boss about how your company could revolutionize the way it does business. I already know you're thinking about making a move—in April 2021, about 4 million people in the United States quit their jobs *voluntarily*. The largest share of them (after retail) were professionals, working in offices, listening to bosses, clocking in at nine and leaving (maybe) by five. I'm willing to bet the top reason they left is because they're unfulfilled. They're searching for something. I don't think the solution can be found in the simple act of quitting. I think what moves people in our modern world of work is the desire to be great. To achieve. To disrupt and stand out.

When you become a Bold One, you find fulfillment. You stop thinking that somewhere else will make you better. You realize that anywhere you go, you can make *it* better.

I hope this book gives you the inspiration, the courage, and the pathway to disrupt *your* field. I want you to feel confident that your ideas are the next big ones. I want you to speak up at your next meeting and offer an insight to your bosses that only you can see. I want you to reinvent your field right where you are, whether in a corporate office or in a coffee shop. I want the incumbents to pay attention to you, the individual, because that's where the next great idea will come from. I want you to become the next Bold One.

Let's get bold.

SECRETS OF THE BOLD ONES

FEED YOUR INSATIABLE NEED TO INNOVATE. Two keys you'll need as you turn these pages. The first, you already have—it's your drive for innovation. Keep it, feed it, and hold on to it.

UNLEASH YOUR HIDDEN TALENT. The second key is what you're doing in the moonlight. Often, your greatest and best skill, your truest talent, isn't the one you're using. To find out where your gift really lies, ask yourself, *What do I do off the clock?* That hidden talent, that quirky idea, is what you'll need to unleash your disruptive DNA.

REMEMBER, ONLY THE BOLD CHANGE THE HISTORY BOOKS. Throughout all of human history, brazen, disruptive individuals, from musicians to scientists, changed the story. Disruptors have always been a little off-kilter. They saw things differently, they thought differently, and they executed, differently. If you want to follow in their footsteps, you've got to be willing to be bold.

UNLOCK YOUR INDIVIDUALITY. Bold *Ones* changed history, not bold *brands*. People follow people, not companies. The next great disruption will come from you—or someone else with a human name. Put your name out there, speak up, act up.

COLLABORATE WITH INCUMBENTS. Bold Ones move independently, but they often work inside of incumbent companies or organizations. By using the individual's tenacity, agility, and fresh outlook, and combining the organization's size, clout, and reputation, bold individuals and large organizations can collaborate on tomorrow's greatest discoveries.

CHAPTER 2

SUCCESS IS A PITFALL

In 2016, *Ebro in the Morning* interviewed a nobody named "Cardi B."[1] Hot 97, which broadcasts the show, is a powerhouse in the world of hip-hop. The show's hosts, Ebro and Rosenberg, are the industry's established sentries. Their word is platinum. One bit of criticism or praise can make or break an artist's career.

At the time, Cardi B's marketability lived in the questionable corners of social media, where her outlandish Instagram posts had landed her a spot on MTV's *Love & Hip Hop: New York*. Apparently, no critic of real clout took Cardi B's music seriously. To them, she was an ex-exotic dancer who spoke poor English, who couldn't rap, and who'd earned a small spotlight on reality TV only because of her cosmetic surgeries. At least that's what Ebro and Rosenberg told her on air.

I've watched the entire 41-minute interview on YouTube. It's uncomfortable.

Ebro and Rosenberg pepper Cardi B with questions about her body parts, her former career as a stripper, and her supposed lack of proper English. To her credit, Cardi B responds patiently, exuding conviction in her thick Bronx accent. When they start discussing her songs, Ebro grunts disapprovingly. Then comes the most damning comment of all. Ebro declares that when it comes to her raps, "We gotta work on that."

Ebro's diss could have ended Cardi B's career right then and there.

But it didn't. Cardi B wouldn't just prove these incumbents wrong. She wouldn't just make it in their world either. She would *remake* their world, and in record time.

In 2017, almost one year to the day after the interview, Cardi B released her first major-label single, "Bodak Yellow." The song garnered critical acclaim, winning various awards, including Single of the Year at the BET Hip Hop Awards and three nominations at the Grammys. Many critics now consider "Bodak Yellow" one of the most influential hip-hop songs of its decade.

By 2018, Cardi B had broken Beyoncé's record for the most simultaneous top-10 songs for a female in her category. By 2019, Cardi B's debut album had made her the first female solo artist in history to win the Grammy Award for Best Rap Album. By 2021, critics mentioned her in the same breath as the greatest female rapper of all time, Lauryn Hill.

Less than a decade into Cardi B's music career, and she already has more sway over hip-hop than the guys who dismissed her.

That's what happens when someone disrupts an industry— when the rules everyone else must follow seem, somehow, not to apply.

When you look up lists of "Greatest Rappers of All Time," you'll likely need to scroll a while on any list until you find a female. Usually the first woman you'll see on the list is Lauryn Hill, from her one studio album in 1998. Since then, if a woman wanted to make it in the rap game, she needed to curate an invite from a male incumbent: Da Brat had Jermaine Dupri; Nicki Minaj had Lil Wayne; Lil' Kim had Notorious B.I.G.

That's why Ebro never saw *her* coming, a woman who didn't attached herself to a man's name. A disruptor who created her own door, disrupted someone else's universe, then left with all the trophies.

SUCCESS IS A PITFALL

The better you are at something, the more likely you are to become the Ebro (aka a doubter) of someone else's innovation tale. Why? Because you've already achieved success one way, and nothing kills innovation like past successes.

Think about how hard leaving success is for you: You know how to land the financing you want. You know how to please the customers in your industry. You understand how to arrange the IT so everything runs smoothly. You're efficient, so in your career, you've built an easy shortcut to what you want, and it's hard to unsee it.

In a scene from the movie *Pearl Harbor*, two officers discuss how safe the military base in Hawaii is. One of them runs through all the reasons their stronghold is impenetrable. But Admiral Kimmel isn't buying it: "The smart enemy attacks you

23

exactly where you think you are safe." Simple but profound. If you start to feel safe like Ebro, you're in trouble. He had everything to lose and nothing to gain by thinking differently, so he didn't bother. He thought he knew exactly how hip-hop worked based on proof from the past.

But past proof doesn't guarantee future success. And companies (especially ones dedicated to excellence) make this exact mistake.

So what do you need to know to make sure your past successes don't hinder your future?

1. **THERE ARE NO BEST PRACTICES.** Don't assume that a solution that worked in the past will work again; think of fresh ideas in every scenario.
2. **DON'T BE AN EBRO EXPERT.** Avoid being defensive about your expertise; instead, take on a rookie mindset.
3. **DON'T FALL INTO THE RUSSELL WESTBROOK TRAP.** Like basketball player Russell Westbrook, it's easy to let past successes define your identity. But this is a trap that hinders your ability to succeed in the future.
4. **GO FROM 100 TO 0 IN SECONDS.** Be willing to start back at the beginning. At zero. As a novice.

Let's dig in.

THERE ARE NO BEST PRACTICES

On the outside, the top management consulting companies rely on supposedly smart, proven tactics to help their clients. After I moved into management consulting at Deloitte, I started coming face-to-face with this one idea frequently: "best practices."

With best practices, you find successful tactics that have been used by others and then help other clients apply them to their own companies. Top firms like McKinsey, BCG, and Bain all use this strategy of repackaging what once worked elsewhere. With a long list of clients and a storied legacy, Deloitte had many of these so-called best practices.

So that's what I offered on all my projects, to all my clients—at first.

But not one of my original initiatives based on best practices ever succeeded. In fact, most of them didn't even attract enough initial interest and traction to properly fail.

One of my early clients was a financial services company that needed to revamp its website and end-to-end digital customer experience. They were looking to shake things up, and they wanted an innovative way for their customers to understand and transact with the company's products and services. I wasn't exactly a customer experience expert, so I did the logical thing: I went through the playbooks Deloitte had issued to other clients to address similar issues. I lifted a success story and then repackaged it. (I literally used the same PowerPoints, processes, and steps.)

Did it work? Not even close.

This client wasn't even interested in trying my "new" idea.

The same story happened with several of my other beginning clients. So, it didn't take long for me to change directions, to start looking at every project as if it were a new beginning, a one-of-a-kind universe with no rules and a blue-sky opportunity. Unsurprisingly, clients started responding, projects started rolling, and innovation started occurring.

Now I'm able to crystallize exactly what Cardi B knew all along: There are no best practices.

DON'T BE AN EBRO EXPERT

There's a fine line between having *excellence* and being an *expert*, but the subtle difference lands you on opposite ends of innovation. Excellence is the pursuit of being best in every situation—something every hardworking, ambitious worker should aspire to. But being an expert with supposed "best practices"? I'll pass.

Zoom out and picture just how Cardi B accomplished what she did.

Before she touched a microphone, she developed a loyal following using social media in the most unconventional way. While other influencers were curating their perfect lives, with filters and aesthetically pleasing grids on Instagram, Cardi B swam in the wrong direction—she went raw, authentic, and unapologetic. She became the anti-Instagram, *on* Instagram. She documented the struggles, the past, and her insane adventures. She stood out in the best way possible. She broke all the "best practices" and had no "expertise." And that's exactly why people loved her, and how she landed a coveted spot on *Love & Hip Hop*.

But Cardi B wasn't about to get stuck in this one success. After her *Ebro in the Morning* appearance, she declined her third-season appearance on *Love & Hip Hop*, going all-in on her music. Seven months later, she had a number one single. It was a pivot for the ages.

She knew not to become the "expert" that Ebro thought he was.

Here's my question: How often do we brush aside the Cardi B moments in our own lives and careers, and opt, instead, to be the Ebro expert?

Consider his arrogance, his matter-of-fact certainty that Cardi B wasn't going anywhere in rap, and ask yourself if you've done the same. Have you dismissed the intern because their idea seemed just a bit too green? When's the last time you internally laughed at someone else's new process because you knew, from experience, it simply wouldn't work?

Ebro had proof. He understood hip-hop. He'd interviewed the greats, and he'd been there at big moments in hip-hop's history. So he felt safe. And that's exactly why he was disrupted. But what if we approached every day like Cardi B instead of Ebro? What if, even within your own specialty, you approached it as if you knew *nothing*? That's the challenge—to walk into the office, and despite years of best practices and prior wins, you walk in as a rookie, a first-timer, who is all-ears for new ideas, who is not just trying to re-create yesterday's success, but who's galvanized thinking about a new future.

That's the Cardi B challenge.

I have a simple hack to use, one that can help you determine if the Ebro mentality has taken up residence in your own mind. Simply ask yourself this question: *Am I defensive about my expertise?*

- If you're an accountant, and you're defensive about the software you use, you're getting close to the Ebro line.
- If you're the software engineer who knows that the Agile method is "always superior," you're setting yourself up for a Cardi B disruption.
- If you're a project manager who understands exactly how to motivate a team, so you do it the same way over and over again, maybe it's time for a new practice.

Defensiveness is the critical component that Ebro was carrying with him. It blinded him to the danger he was in. He felt comfortable, reassured, safe. Yet, he was anything but safe.

If you're utterly certain about how to accomplish a project, which software to use, or what methods are superior, to the point that you're defensive of those practices, you're ripe for an Ebro awakening. Cardi B never had time to defend her expert status. The moment she did well in one arena, she disrupted herself.

By definition, an expert is someone who knows how to do something well *based on experience*. Disruption, by definition, revels in the new, dabbles in the upside down, and dares to think differently. Bold Ones are courageous enough, and willing enough, to bounce from one idea to the next.

If you want the same haircut, you don't want a disruptor; you want a process follower. You'll get exactly what you had last time. But if you want a fashion-busting, trend-leading style, you've got to look your hairstylist in the eye, trust what will happen, and leap.

If something's "standard" or "best practice," you might as well say, "We're on the downturn." If you perform your design job the same way you did 10 years ago, you're likely about to be replaced. If you project-manage your team using the same processes you used five years prior, your teammates may not be listening. If you approach problems with the same mindset you accessed five minutes ago, I promise you, you're starting to become an expert, ripe for disruption.

Don't be an Ebro expert.

DON'T FALL INTO THE RUSSELL WESTBROOK TRAP

There's a reason we all have such a problem letting go of old tools, methodologies, and processes. They worked.

We're all addicted to success. Failure feels awful, while winning feels good. We'll take a quick, small win over a giant risk any day. In fact, we're so excited about the feeling of winning, we'll sacrifice true accomplishments for a mirage of it. Don't believe me? Look no further than NBA player Russell Westbrook.

Westbrook is a former MVP and the triple-double king of the NBA.[2] He had 194 triple-doubles by the time I started this book. No other basketball player can touch that statistic.

He's one of my favorite athletes to watch, playing with incredible intensity, barreling down the court with electrifying dunks. Watch him play, basketball fan or not, and you'll think, *He's the best on the floor.* And he'll likely dazzle the commentators with his stats.

But those stats never translate to *wins*.

In fact, teams can't get rid of Westbrook fast enough. He's been moved from Oklahoma City to Houston to Washington to Los Angeles—all within three years.

The problem isn't that he's not good. The problem is that he *was* good. His style was successful for the Oklahoma City Thunder. There he gained such a badass reputation that he hasn't been able to let go of his old style. He isn't willing to try something new that will tarnish his stats. The risk is just too great. Apparently he'd rather lose games as long as his numbers tell him he's doing well.

Overall, his identity is wrapped up in triple-doubles. It's like he's getting style points for his breaststroke but he's getting lapped in the pool. I call this the Russell Westbrook Trap—an unwillingness to let go of identity.

One of my mentors and favorite ex-partners at Deloitte, Paul-Marc Frenette, used the following words when talking with oil executives. He'd tell them—to their face—you guys are so "fat, rich, and lazy that you can't see the future." (Yeah, Paul-Marc was a gangster.)

Individuals and entire companies fall into the Russell Westbrook Trap. Old bands keep coming back for "reunion tours." Once-retired athletes keep coming back for an encore. Movie studios get one hit, and three sequels later, we're seeing commercials for *Fast and the Furious 34.*

And the more successful you once were, the nastier the teeth of your own personal Russell Westbrook Trap.

In a now-famous paper, researcher Karl E. Weick identified firefighters who died while holding onto their tools. Tragically, in the fires he studied, Weick observed that many firefighters would have lived if they'd simply dropped the bulky equipment they were carrying. Instead, they ran holding weighty hoses, axes, and gear, which slowed them down so much they couldn't escape the engulfing flames. Weick concluded his paper by proposing that the tools—which the experienced firefighters had once successfully used to put out other fires—had seared themselves into the psyche of the men to the degree that they considered those tools as extensions of their self-images.

Spielberg, one of the greatest filmmakers of all time, once got so mad that a new web-only studio—Netflix—was sweeping the Oscars that he suggested that the Academy shouldn't allow Netflix to compete against him. Even the GOAT[3] filmmaker had become a bit "fat, rich, and lazy."

The more successful your former tools, techniques, and ideas were, the more they become ingrained in your own mind, until, eventually, you see these as part of you. To stop working the way you did previously would mean you'd become someone new (or so you think).

LET GO OF STATUS

Our identity is built not only upon the tools and methodologies of yesteryear, but on the status we receive from previous accomplishments. When others congratulate us on our projects, we want to repeat the action. When we work hard to ace a class, our GPA reflects an uptick, and we want to repeat the action.

Status is embedded in our DNA. When we win, others notice, we notice, and our status with our coworkers, our company, and our industries rises. Our brain says, *That feels good.* In his 1992 *Class: A Guide Through the American Status System*, Paul Fussell discusses how losing your current level of status is one of the greatest fears for any person in society. Russell Westbrook may not be winning games, but he does get to hear "triple-double" all the time. Giving that up isn't easy.

In your own world, you must proactively decouple your psyche from the status that is so alluring, particularly as you gain success. When I say "proactively," I mean it. If you want to practice disrupting yourself, then start by intentionally reducing your own status.

I assume you're excellent within your career. Likely, you've earned some sort of accreditation that suggests as much: MBA, PMP, CFA, CPA, etc. These sit on our résumés, on our LinkedIn descriptions, and on our bios. They may be appropriate in those settings, but don't let these letters attach themselves to your identity. Personally, I try to prevent having any designations beside my name. It's just too easy to carry them as if they defined me. Plus, they intimidate others, or, at best, repel great ideas. If Ebro had been less of an expert and relied less on his own status, maybe *he* would have been the one to launch Cardi B's hip-hop career. Instead of mocking her, he might have recognized that she was the next big thing.

Here's the antidote to the identity and status temptation of the Russell Westbrook Trap: Get low on the totem pole. Whatever's laying hold to your identity, *lose it*. Let go of the ego, and with it, all the status. You may have found out how to master yesterday's methodologies, last year's software, or your company's politics. But those are stats. Are you—and your coworkers—winning games?

Status is alluring. Success lays hold onto your identity. To keep yourself free of the Russell Westbrook Trap, here are a few tactics:

- **PLACE YOURSELF IN "LOWER-STATUS" SITUATIONS.** Come off the bench. Clean the floors. Be the assistant. Fetch your team's coffee. Be the team's driver. Take the middle seat. Take the bus. Greet the members of your team at the door. Deliver them lunch. Wherever you are on the totem pole—whether intern or CXO— go *down* the pole. There's a heap of benefits to these practices—if nothing else, you'll learn that your identity isn't wrapped up in hierarchy.
- **SUBSTITUTE STORY FOR TITLES.** Look, I get it. You worked hard for that degree (or that title in your company), but is that *really* the key that will unlock future innovation in your field? Try this instead: The next time you introduce yourself in the office, at a work lunch, or at a conference, drop the title, the school, or the big-name company you worked for. Instead, tell a story about what you (and optimally, your team) *did*. Stats are cute. Wins are hot.

- **LISTEN TO THE NEW KID.** What if Westbrook were willing to watch younger players—and even *learn* from them? When you detach from your learned expertise, letting go of your identity, you'll learn something new. The next time the intern, the inexperienced, or the hotshot shows up with a unique, even crazy, idea, listen. Sure, they may be green. But maybe they're onto something.

- **WATCH THE MARKETPLACE.** Every day, innovators are shipping hot software, new services, and hip products. Sign up, dabble on the fringes, and tinker in the latest. This will keep you inspired and fresh. There are a few hot communities where hip innovators connect to share their latest and greatest—one of my favorites is ProductHunt.com.

GO FROM 100 TO 0 IN SECONDS

Maybe you're thinking, *I'm not an expert at all*. Well, you're probably not tempted by the Russell Westbrook Trap (yet).

But the question for everyone—from the experienced to the novice—is simple:

Are you willing to constantly start at the bottom, at zero?

Disruption requires execution into the unknown, a faithful leap into something that you've never tried before. Baby steps—like listening to others and letting go of ego—are just that, baby steps. But when it comes time to jump, like Cardi B, you've got to be willing to be at the bottom. If you want to invent an entirely new product, you must be willing to know nothing about it. To create a new software program, you must experiment. To pioneer a new workplace culture, be willing to be wrong, a lot.

Incremental improvement is easy—you get to build on a foundation that already exists. But to start a company, build a new product, pitch a client in a new way, or forge a new line of business, you've got to be willing to start at the bottom, at nothing.

No one knows this better than producer Jermaine Dupri.

In 1990, Dupri noticed two kids, both named Chris, at Greenbriar Mall in Atlanta. They seemed like they were already celebrities—girls were commenting about their looks, and they had an aura of fame about them. He watched as they went up to a cookie counter, and the young ladies went wild for them, even giving them free cookies. By this time, Dupri was in the music industry, but he'd only collaborated with women, and he'd obviously never heard these kids sing, nor did he know if they even could. He'd never worked with men—not that they were truly "men" yet—they were only 12 and 13 years old. Still, Dupri *did* know these Chrises had some sort of "it" factor. So he gave them his number and told them he wanted to make them stars.

Less than two years later, they went multi-platinum under the name Kriss Kross.

Then Dupri did it again with female rap group Xscape, whose first album also went platinum. Next stop? Da Brat: platinum. In 1995, Dupri collaborated with Mariah Carey on a little song called "Always Be My Baby": triple platinum. Usher, Destiny's Child, Jay-Z, Lil' Bow Wow, and Weezer all have one thing in common—Dupri.

Dupri talks about going from 100 to 0. Every time he scoops up a fledgling artist or collaborates with a star on a new song, he never views the experience as something to which he's bringing expertise. Instead, he views it as his opportunity to start brand new, from the ground up, reducing himself to zero. While everyone else is trying to build on where they were yesterday, Dupri actively looks for the opportunity to start over. That mentality has allowed him to continually rethink hip-hop and R&B. Now he's going into vegan ice cream (true story). Will it work? I don't know. And that's the point.

Staying at 90 and trying to move to 100 is the easy choice. Relying on best practices is the cop-out. Bold Ones take the risk, and they're willing to be a rookie in a new endeavor. While everyone else wants to go from 0 to 100, Bold Ones have the guts to attempt Dupri's 100 to 0.

An ancient Haitian proverb says, "Behind mountains are more mountains." There's always a new mountain available. If you haven't found the top of one yet—start moving. But once you get there, recognize there's another one out there, and to get to that one, you must descend into a valley. To find the new, you must constantly leave the high to embrace the low. Are you willing to travel the valleys, to restart, to reinvent, to be a novice, to fail, all the way back to zero?

I think there are three ways we can embrace this 100-to-0 mentality.

1. IDENTIFY YOUR NEXT MOUNTAIN

Bold Ones are willing to reduce themselves to zero, only because they have that next mountain in view. Dupri doesn't drop down to nothing just for the sake of it—he's eyeing the next prize. And every mountain is a newer, bigger one.

Identifying where you want to go is key. If Westbrook would visualize winning, he might be willing to give up his status as the triple-double king in exchange for a championship. So before you decide to dive down to zero, ask yourself, *What's worth going from 100 down to the bottom?*

I get to speak with a lot of people across the globe who want to be doing something different than what they're doing currently. They want to dabble in something new. They're in accounting, but they want to be in blockchain. They're financial advisors who are really storytellers. They're CXOs at traditional firms, but they have wild ideas about their industry. They all tell me they desire to do something different. I tell them to make it concrete, real, to paint that next picture clear in their head. Dream up that mountain.

2. INCH TOWARD THAT MOUNTAIN

Actively identify where you want to be; then get a little flirty with it. You don't need to change your job tomorrow, or present your hot new idea straight to your firm's CEO. Instead, dabble, play, experiment. Give yourself some small wins. Later you can go bigger.

Start by actively learning skills exactly in what you're interested in. Today there's a new skill site for just about anything. If you're a basketball player who wants to code, go to CodeAcademy.com. If you're a coder who wants to learn basketball, go to MasterClass and learn from Steph Curry. Likewise for almost every imaginable skill, hobby, or idea—someone's started the community for it already. Hop on board.

There may be other small moves you can make today—maybe you need to save up financially so you can start your own firm. Perhaps you want to move up in your company and you need a mentor. Take some action, anything, every week toward those goals. Be willing to work for free on nights and weekends to learn a new craft. Skip eating out to start putting some money away to save up for your own company. Whatever you must do, inch your way up the mountain.

3. USE TRAGEDY TO START OVER

I find one of the easiest and most practical ways of going from 100 to 0 is to seize moments afforded by tragedy.

When my father passed, I had to take over his accounting clients—starting at zero.

When the pandemic hit and all my speaking engagements were canceled, I called my team and asked how we could re-create the best livestream experience anyone has ever seen—starting at zero.

When you're looking for somewhere to start with disruption, look no further than your next tragedy or upset. These are the moments when you can ask yourself, nearly risk-free, "If I were starting from zero, how would we start this?"

EBRO'S ERROR

If you walk into Ebro's studio, you'll catch a laid-back, T-shirt–wearing, hip-hop aficionado, a tattooed host who says what he thinks, plays what he wants, and rubs elbows with the gods of the hip-hop universe. A true rebel in loud, irreverent tones. *This man, you'd think, answers to no one.* The same guy that was in the studio the day Cardi B walked in.

But then, even with all his rabble-rousing, Ebro had become a slow-moving has-been incumbent, with old tools, outdated practices, and stale ideas, whose opinion was ultimately dismissed by someone *he* was trying to wave off, someone who would change his universe. He was the gatekeeper of a world he didn't understand anymore. Once upon a time, his mindset had perhaps forged the path from zero to hero in the rap game. But by sticking to his guns and traversing the one path he knew, he missed who would become one of his industry's greatest.

Copycatting what worked before doesn't work.

Be willing to do what's new, even if what you're doing is currently working. Go from 100, to zero.

SECRETS OF THE BOLD ONES

REMEMBER, THERE ARE NO BEST PRACTICES. You cannot templatize success, or masquerade innovation in incremental changes. Innovation is, by definition, turning to the new. If it worked yesterday, it's not disruptive.

DON'T BE AN EBRO EXPERT. If you're getting defensive about your ideas, then you're slipping into the fallacy of expertise. Bold Ones are willing to constantly be the rookie and to listen to rookies. They're willing to give up their expertise to embrace new mindsets, ideas, methodologies, tools, and tactics.

DON'T FALL INTO THE RUSSELL WESTBROOK TRAP, WHERE SUCCESS AND STATUS ATTACH THEMSELVES TO YOUR IDENTITY. The more successful we were yesterday, and the more others congratulate us for that, the less willing we'll be to disrupt ourselves. You must proactively detach your identity from your status and your previous tools. Drop the fancy titles, tell stories, and look for ways to lower yourself in the hierarchy.

ALWAYS BE WILLING TO START BACK OVER AT ZERO. They know there's always another, higher mountain, and to get there, they have to leave today's successes. Importantly, you must identify what it is you're actively moving toward. Then, at least weekly, move toward it.

CHAPTER 3

CHIPPING TOWARD YOUR NEXT BIG MOVE

In May 2015, ESPN fired sportswriter, editor, and podcast host Bill Simmons. The company considered him "disrespectful." He'd argued with his bosses, provoked controversial attention, and even publicly bashed the NFL commissioner. Oh, and *then* he dared ESPN to fire him over it.

ESPN took him up on that dare and let him go.

It was a $200 million mistake.

Simmons had spent 15 years at ESPN, cultivating fresh journalistic ideas, challenging incumbent thinking about impartiality, and stoking passions with his contentious writing and podcast. Nothing was traditional about Simmons. In addition to his radical use of language, he never minded giving particular attention to his favorite Bostonian sports teams, and he wasn't shy about his personal life.

Simmons had talked ESPN into giving him substantial freedom to operate his own multimedia website, Grantland, a brand that lived under the ESPN umbrella and specialized in long-form sports journalism.

A few months after ESPN canned Simmons, they shut down the entire Grantland project—it was notoriously expensive, as Simmons demanded only the best writers and editors for the website. From day one, it had struggled to turn a profit. So less than six months after tossing Simmons, ESPN announced they would be retiring his brainchild.

But Simmons believed in the journalism and audience he'd cultivated. So, soon after he left, he resurrected the concept in the form of a new company, The Ringer, which was essentially Grantland 2.0. Simmons kept all his rebellious style, used a similar tone and vibe, and even swiped many of the same ESPN writers and editors he'd previously worked with. But he wasn't done poking fun at his former employer. In one of The Ringer's first pieces, Simmons offered *his* version of the highly publicized breakup he'd had with ESPN. True to form, he held nothing back, even jokingly suggesting that his new media company should be officially titled "F*ck Off, ESPN."

Today sports fans across the globe tune in to download podcast episodes and articles from The Ringer. Personally, I never miss an episode of his show, *The Bill Simmons Podcast*, an unapologetic and honest take on sports and pop culture.

Simmons has always been brash and unafraid to challenge, and never has been willing to sit inside the rules. He's bold. And, even when ESPN bailed out on his concept after four years, Simmons kept going on the same trajectory.

If you're going to be a Bold One, you've got to get a new pair of specs, ones that allow you to see the coming disruption. Not only that, but you've got to find a way to hang on to that perspective even when the environment gets rocky, others laugh at you, or no one understands. Let's get you those new glasses.

YOUR NEW GLASSES

Simmons wasn't able to disrupt sports journalism simply because he's a witty writer or podcast host. He observed and accurately dissected the shifting cultural waters in the mainstream marketplace. Then he took his own surfboard and positioned it to catch the waves.

He accurately understood that the world wanted sports media to be more opinionated, open, and real. ESPN, like other sports media outlets, had capitulated to a more traditional sentiment, where "fair" and "unbiased" ruled the day. But Simmons played a hunch, believing that people wanted authenticity, real opinions, and something to challenge their intellect.

In this chapter, we're going to explore how to avoid the catastrophes of shortsightedness. Particularly, I'm going to help you take some steps *outside* of where you are currently in your career, whether as a journalist, a barista, or a project manager, to understand the world through a more holistic lens.

We're going to look at:

1. **THE ILLUSION OF THE CORE.** We've been told to double down on what we're best at. So most of us have been focusing all our efforts and development on a select few skills. But to stay relevant, we must understand where

the world is going and be willing to move beyond our own "core capabilities" and add new skills and tools.

2. **DENTING THE OUTSIDE.** We can expand our perspective and capabilities by simply "chipping away"—placing small bets on ourselves by learning and experimenting. We don't have to make monstrous moves today, but we must always keep moving.

3. **THE 3% RULE.** To be disruptive, we don't have to invent a new product, service, or method all at once. Instead, we can remix current ideas, process, and technologies, then sprinkle on just 3 percent of our own style to create something new.

4. **WHY IT'S OK TO BE WASTEFUL.** The professional world is hyperfocused on efficiency. The problem? We aren't willing to explore. If we want to discover something new, we must be willing to tinker, explore, and be wasteful.

The aim of this chapter is to equip you with the tools necessary to see the world as Simmons saw it. And that starts by scaling over one specific roadblock: your own core capabilities.

THE ILLUSION OF THE CORE

Illusions work on a simple premise—distraction. A good illusionist forces your focus on what their hands are doing, or on the loud sound that originates in another part of the room, or on an ostentatious painting. The illusionist wants your focus anywhere but *where the magic's actually happening.*

For an illusionist, a distraction is the perfect mechanism to dazzle audiences. For the rest of us, it's the perfect obstacle to disruption. The illusion that captivates many of us in the marketplace isn't a rabbit coming out of a hat or someone being sawed in half; it's what I call the "Illusion of the Core."

The "core" is your supposed awe-inspiring super-ability. We're told to focus on that "one area" of skills or expertise. Our specialty, our core. For each of us, our specialty may differ, but from the time we graduate college and throughout our careers, we're supposed to hone our craft, double down, and stay in our lane. The intention may be good, and there's clearly wisdom in focus, but if we're not careful, we'll fall into a trap, one where we hyperfocus only on a niche, missing where the world's going, or our own unique skill set. We tend to think:

"I'm a journalist, so I write stories."
"I'm an accountant, so I use Excel."
"I'm a salesperson, so I talk to people."

These mental equations make sense temporarily. But they also can get you stuck. A journalist is more than a writer, an accountant is more than an Excel expert, and a salesperson is more than a talker.

Institutions often take the same approach, focusing on their core product, audience, or segment. Again, there's power in focus. But as we learned in Chapter 2 with the example of the firefighters, a narrow focus on a particular set of tools, methods, or process can actually be problematic. And in this case, not only does this illusion make us biased toward traditional methods (which was the problem with Ebro), but it can also cause us to focus on the here and now far too much, instead of putting on our long-view glasses.

The upside of narrowing your focus on your core is that you can increase a particular set of muscles and capabilities, whether in a technology, a skill set, or a methodology. But the downside is that when we narrow our focus, we think small. And when we think small, we lose sight of the overarching mission. Let me give you an example.

At Deloitte, I once hired someone that another office thought was just a notch too different. As one of the leaders of innovation in our region, I'd earned a reputation for always recruiting top, innovative, and "unique" talent. One day, a senior manager in our Calgary office sent me a message. Apparently, the people there had interviewed someone they *liked*, but they simply couldn't hire him because, in their words, he was "too innovative."

Too innovative? I thought. I had to meet this guy, whom we'll call Jack.

Once I met Jack, I could confirm—he was different. He didn't focus on the charismatic selling qualities that most top management consulting firms look for in consultants: At the time, he couldn't carry a room with his panache, and his argument didn't always resonate at a deep level. Most interviewers, like my Calgary colleagues, didn't see a star-power consultant.

But that was the short view. They were missing something else: Jack was wickedly interested in a budding technology, 3D printing. My team, always on the lookout for what's on the horizon, hired him. We weren't quite sure what we'd do with him, but he was on the fringe, right where we wanted to be.

He proved to be an invaluable asset. Of course, he brought his unique building capabilities and 3D printing knowledge into our wheelhouse, helping the firm create deliverables that it had never built before.

The other office was too focused on the core of what they did well, and they weren't willing to look outside it. What Jack did—3D printing—certainly wasn't a core need for my team; I didn't quite know how Jack would be valuable, but I'd been on the fringe long enough to know I wanted to be in the room when "different" people succeeded.

A BOLD QUESTION

Innovation starts by asking ourselves a deep question. One that requires a broad view, to get our eyes off our own core and consider the broader marketplace. We've got to ask ourselves one deep, scary question:

Where is the world going?

That's the jump-start, the catalyst to moving outside your core.

It's not a safe question; in fact, the answer might move us in ways we never thought. Too many people and companies want to take the distraction, the bait, to continue living in the *Matrix* and believing that the world isn't changing, and that their core will protect them.

If we want to avoid the ESPN mistake, we've got to ask ourselves this dangerous question *today*.

So let's ask that question now and shift back to looking at ourselves. Start peeling back the layers in your own career: Where are you burying your head in the sand as the world is changing? Are you focusing *too much* on what you (or others) have told you is your own core?

As you think through this, keep in mind that *authenticity to yourself* is key. In fact, it's *vital*. What if Jack had said, "I'm a consultant; in the consulting world, to be successful, I need to drop my obsession with 3D printing and refocus on what matters"? If Jack had focused on what was supposedly the most important, central aspects of being a business consultant, he would have missed the wave that he was set up to take. Likely, if he'd diverted his time and energy into becoming a better consultant, he would have probably landed a job with the other team, and mine never would have hired him.

But Jack didn't get caught up in a narrow, simplified version of himself. Instead, he kept all his uniqueness and his long view. He knew that his unique interests were a particular match for the coming world, and ultimately he never needed to negotiate on that.

So when you ask, "Where is the world going?" don't abandon what you love; instead, determine how your wildest idea may be the perfect asset to a new revolution.

INCREASE YOUR SURFACE AREA OF EXPLORATION

So how do you avoid getting so focused on what you're doing that you miss the waves of innovation?

You've got to have enough input into your life, enough ideas circulating, and enough channels of information, that there's a constant flow. You can't get dissuaded by your role, company, or even country.

To avoid the hypnotic effect of the Illusion of the Core, get comfortable walking into the jungle of uncertainty. Find the fringe and dabble. You know that new decentralized platform or obscure technology that's made you think *This may be the next big thing,* but you haven't really looked into because it's scary or intimidating? Why not learn about it? Get in the Reddit forums and be part of the conversation. Ask questions; dig in.

Is there a new way of thinking, a new process, a new development method that seems fringe? Read the Twitter threads; listen to the podcasts; be willing to double-click on the strange new technology, the odd social media network, or the intimidating new method. Utilize podcasts, books, YouTube videos, whatever you can. While it may not apply directly to what you're doing now, you need to have a surface area that always allows for "the new."

Look in the darkness, and never reject disruptive ideas. The dumber it sounds, the more value there may be. You'll find that most disruptive ideas that are worth experimenting start in the loneliest places—basements, Starbucks coffee shops, the subreddits, and private Slack groups.

Above all, always consider where culture is going, and what skills, assets, network, and understanding you must cultivate today, so that when tomorrow's fringe culture arrives—and it will—not only will you be unsurprised, but you may just be part of it.

PLAY THE HUNCHES

While Simmons had his eyes wide open to the cultural moment of the internet, he wasn't exactly sure how it was going to play out. Likewise, my team didn't know exactly what we'd do with Jack, but we knew we wanted him.

If you're going to disrupt, to innovate, you've got to be willing to execute on the hunches.

What if you bet on that hunch you've had for a while about how consumer behavior is going to change? Maybe your team's been marketing in a specific way to a specific demographic, but your gut is telling you that there's a bigger market in a different age group or a different category. Maybe you've had a hunch, for a while, that you need to develop a partnership with a rising star—an employee or a business—that's doing some creative things in the market, but you haven't reached out because your own built-in fears said, *That's not my core.* Well, overcome that reaction, and play your hunch. Reach out; make the partnership; change the game. If you're wrong, you've just exercised your muscle for the next innovation.

DENTING THE OUTSIDE

In 2022, I had a few consulting sessions with Walmart executives. Remember, this company has been wildly successful since its founding in 1962. I was brought in to help consult on one of its future innovation strategies. Explaining to the folks at a 60-year-old retail company that they need to look outside their core of inexpensive retail at brick-and-mortar isn't exactly an easy sell. But I still made the move.

I inched them into the idea, without dropping a bomb. Instead of telling them to make insane moves immediately, I told them to think small and just start making little moves outside their core. I encouraged chipping, learning, understanding the broader marketplace and cultural shifts. I explained that they could experiment later, and eventually, once a certain experiment started working, they could take a leap.

In my talks, I call this process "denting the outside": a subtle chipping away at the outside of your own core of expertise. The goal is to eventually break through to connect yourself and your skill sets with the jet stream of disruption. Disruption is all about becoming the Bold One, the lone base jumper in a plane full of traditionalists. But—and here's the key—you don't base-jump before you learn how to skydive. And you don't skydive without taking a class. It's baby steps all along the way.

In your career, you take where you are today, and you start inching outside your core, denting it, slowly chipping away.

Making the move into a full-time innovation strategist and speaker wasn't an overnight accomplishment for me. If I'd told my wife one night over pillow talk, "Hey babe, I'm going to quit my job as a 12-year veteran employee tomorrow to start advising companies on disruption," I probably wouldn't be writing this book. Even if I weren't scared to make the move, she would have been.

So I just dented: I moved from accounting into consulting within my own institution, Deloitte. There I started stretching my innovation wings. From that position, I started speaking on innovation *outside* my company. When I had some proof of my ideas, I was able to convince my wife of my plan to branch out on my own. This bore some risk, but I wasn't betting our entire financial future.

It works the same way with your bosses, and with an entire organization. If you're interested in a new space, and you think your team, department, or company should consider altering its course, go get some real-world experience; then come back and *show* people. "I really think Web3 is going to make a splash. Here's a small side project I've been tinkering on . . ." is a lot more persuasive than trying to convince a team of traditionalists that because some kids in their garage are really onto something, they should change their entire course today.

If you want to dent the outside, you've got to get past the immune systems—yours, and others'.

In summary, start small. To bypass the immune system problem—of yours or anyone else's—make mini-bets. Movement is the key, not perfection. You don't need to constantly take insane bets, but you do need to be constantly exercising your innovation muscle. Specifically, there are two keys that can help you begin to execute as quickly as possible:

KEY 1. THINK ABOUT THE NEXT RING

In the 1930s, a Russian psychologist named Lev Vygotsky started developing a model based on his interactions with children. He posited that there are three areas of a learner's abilities:

1. **WHAT IS KNOWN.** This is the center ring, what you already know how to do quite well. This circle represents what a learner can do without help.
2. **ZONE OF PROXIMAL DEVELOPMENT.** In the second ring, a learner can complete tasks *with help*, and the assumption is that this zone will eventually become part of the learner's core.
3. **WHAT IS UNKNOWN.** In the outermost circle lies what is unknown, that a learner would have a hard time completing even with help, as this area is entirely outside the person's understanding.

If we think about moving *adjacent* to our core, we can often start to make moves without having to jump to what's totally unknown. Simmons went from writing to podcasting at one point, a big jump, but not a crazy one. It's an adjacent skill, incorporating his brash personality and partiality to biased storytelling. Cardi B went from stripping to reality TV, but in between, she used her Instagram—a visual venue, like exotic dancing—to gain an audience. With an audience, reality TV makes sense. There she started talking and gaining support for her latest hot venture, rap. Cardi B was always moving, but she wasn't always betting the farm. She was moving adjacent to her current skills, enlarging—and eventually disrupting—her entire core. It's the dance between boldness and utter brashness.

If you're a software engineer who wants to be a writer, start with *technical* writing. If you're a general contractor who wants to get into software, why not start by developing a scheduling app for your team? Small, adjacent moves gain buy-in, and they're often the easiest, quick wins.

KEY 2. DEFAULT TO TEAM STRATEGY

Once you've convinced yourself to take chances, convincing others to join you is generally the next move you should make. While branching could be the best-case scenario for some (or at some point), in many cases, the best outcomes include a Bold One collaborating with a company.

Yes, Simmons made $200 million. But ESPN hasn't since totally collapsed. It still owns sports and has an audience size that Simmons, even now, could only dream of. What if they'd worked together? How much more successful could they both be today? With ESPN's network, reach, and decades of hard-earned name-brand recognition and Simmons's creativity and boldness, their combined output could have exceeded $200 million.

I did eventually leave Deloitte, but I loved my time there, and I still have contacts in the firm I work with today. And remember: to become the godfather of the PlayStation, Kutaragi never had to leave.

Don't default to leaving. Default to collaborating.

YOUR NEW CORE

When we open our eyes to the processes, methods, and technologies others are using, we can often see efficiencies and breakthroughs that we can bring into our own core competency and, in turn, disrupt our industries. That's one alternative, but it's almost the lowest-level alternative. When you dent *outside* your core, you may just discover something so profound, so interesting, and so compelling to you, that you aren't just going to bring it inside your core. You're going to make it your new core. And that's perhaps the largest reason everyone must dabble on the outside: You don't know yourself well enough until you move outside your comfort zone.

You may rediscover your own capabilities. Previously, you were a salesperson, but after you dent the outside, you find out there's more to the story. Yesterday you were an editor, but after denting, you know there's something else more powerful inside.

The world's waiting.
Don't wait to dent outside your core.

THE 3% RULE

One way to innovate is to simply *remix.*

A remix in innovation is exactly what it is in music: a reorganization of ingredients already produced. You reformulate them, and then add in your own flare to create something just new enough that it's innovative, but just classic enough that it's possible. You wondering, *How much of my own flare do I need to add to call it innovative?* Well, it turns out, there's an exact number: 3 percent. It's a concept developed by the late Virgil Abloh, creator of the high-fashion label Off-White.

"Three percent is intentional . . . experimental. . . . It's a parting from the structures designed to inhibit or constrain," he wrote in *Domus 1060*. "Three percent gave us Picasso in his African period. In the same way that it gave us J Dilla and the hip-hop movement that raised me."[1]

Abloh was the first African American to become an artistic director at a *French* luxury fashion house (Louis Vuitton), and apparently his 3% Rule took him there. Few industries rely on appearing "fresh" as much as Abloh's, but by looking at the world only slightly differently, he put giant holes inside of handbags and turned graphic tees into high fashion. *Time* named him as one of the 100 most influential people on earth.

It turns out, 3 percent is just enough.

You can find examples of how Bold Ones have executed the 3% Rule everywhere; they remix prior innovations with just enough of their own style to create a modern disruption. To land on the moon, humanity flew through thousands of years of breakthroughs in computing and in our understanding of gravity and the universe. Neil Armstrong's famous "small step" line was truly prophetic: Take a small step today that builds on the greatness of others.

Here are two ideas to help you foster a "3%," small-step mentality.

1. COMBINE TECH, PROCESSES, AND MARKETS

Maybe you're a healthcare professional, and you stumble on cryptocurrency. Is there a way you can combine healthcare and crypto to do something disruptive in patient privacy? Perhaps you're a regional marketing manager and you stumble on the

Agile process used in software—is it possible to apply this methodology to re-create marketing campaigns? If you're a social worker who understands that the world is becoming more data-driven—is there a way to connect data to your community to address domestic violence?

2. LOOK OUTSIDE TO SOLVE INTERNAL PROBLEMS

Henry Ford stole the idea for his famous assembly line from a meatpacking warehouse. More recently, Steve Jobs stole the idea for his world-renowned Apple store layout by witnessing a Ritz Carlton hotel lobby.

What's going on outside your company and your industry that you could utilize? The connections are not always obvious at first, and they don't have to be. When Kara Goldin, founder of Hint Water, broke off from Silicon Valley after creating a $1 billion segment of AOL's business, she brought her former skill set of collaboration. When she couldn't find the chemical answer she needed to change the way infused water stays fresh, she looked around and asked questions, knowing someone would help her. The industry was averse to collaboration, but Goldin was from tech, where collaboration abounded. Sure enough, she found someone willing to share an idea on how to infuse water with natural flavors and maintain freshness.

In your current role, if you're facing a problem, is the exact tool, methodology, or process you need found *outside* your role, in another marketplace? If you're a factory manager, learn from technologists. If you're a project manager for app development, look to what's going on in mechanical engineering; if you're a graphic designer, maybe your next breakthrough will be found by studying an assembly line.

WHY IT'S OK TO BE WASTEFUL

In business, we've grown accustomed to the "zero-waste" mantra. It's encoded in our ethos.

As far as sustainability is concerned, I get it. But when the zero-waste philosophy drips into the way we think about our time, energy, money, and resources at a business, there's a costly side effect: Without waste, we destroy the possibility of innovation.

Waste is *essential* to innovation, because experimentation is essential to innovation.

The path of the status quo is very efficient. It's a deeply outlined, guarded, and well-trodden path from one end of the forest to the other. We all know where to start, and how to get to the end, efficiently, without wasting a single movement. But innovation requires a jaunt down off the trail, to find "something else." Often we don't even know what we're looking for. You just know it's in the woods, somewhere.

In 2021, Beeple sold his magnum opus, an NFT mosaic of thousands of small squares, for more than $69 million. The mosaic, entitled Everydays, is a purely digital file, composed of 5,000 squares of artwork. The sale crushed all previous records for NFT sales, and it was the first time a large auction house had auctioned purely digital artwork. But Beeple's move wasn't a steady, incremental climb. He was making small squares every day, then putting them into a larger collage.

On the one hand, it was a purely wasteful venture. On the other hand, it made him millions.

If he had had a boss, I wonder if they would have told him to "stop being wasteful."

Lionel Messi, one of the greatest soccer players in history, said it like this: "It took me 17 years and 114 days to become an overnight success." Readiness for a big innovation requires constant practice on smaller ones; in other words, you've got to experiment—and be a little wasteful. Kick the soccer ball around.

The inherent problem with experimentation is that, *most* of the time, you're actually losing, or at least not gaining. Messi wasn't getting a percentage of his success in down payments. Beeple wasn't seeing a small amount of his eventual $69 million. More like it's all a seeming waste, then a sudden smash hit.

You find success by traveling along a trail of failures. Be willing to make numerous mistakes in search of that one big hit. Try, fail, laugh, get up, and move on.

Grantland struggled in its infancy to make money. ESPN was seemingly justified in shutting it down. But Simmons resurrected the idea, because he wasn't just thinking about tomorrow's profits. He was considering the distant future. He was engaging with the undercurrents that were building, that no one could yet see.

In a world of ESPNs, be a Bill Simmons.

SECRETS OF THE BOLD ONES

BE WARY OF THE ILLUSION OF THE CORE. The greatest threats to the long view are "core" capabilities, as people (and companies) tend to hyperfocus on their role or central offering. Instead of narrowing your vision, expand it. Understand broader technological trends, global shifts, and evolving public perceptions. Be ready to connect your truest, deepest skills with disruptive ideas. Join the conversations on the fringes and double-click on hot new ideas.

DENT THE OUTSIDE. Institutions and individuals have immune systems that immediately attempt to reject large-scale disruption. Just because you can't leap today doesn't mean you shouldn't be moving. If you're wanting to disrupt book publishing, you don't have to announce it today, but you do need to be in the conversation, making small bets on yourself until it's time to dive in full bore.

USE THE 3% RULE TO REMIX. Just 3 percent is enough to change the game. The most disruptive players in every industry—whether fashion, technology, or the arts—build on the innovations of others. They remix ideas from multiple industries, bring in concepts from other countries, and then sprinkle on 3 percent of their own magic to create disruption.

BE WASTEFUL. Often, we're so focused on efficiency, we aren't willing to try what isn't a sure bet. By definition, anything that's disruptive is new—it's likely untested. As a result, many disruptive ideas are "wasteful," not ever materializing or leading to demonstrable gains immediately. However, if we want to win long-term, we *must* explore, try new things, and be willing to experiment in ways that are not surefire wins.

CHAPTER 4

PARADOX OF PIRACY

I f you've ever thought your past—whether personal or professional—is the barrier to your individual future, read on.

Our next Bold One was never accepted into a highbrow university, and most think she couldn't even read or write. In fact, her first profession was probably the oldest one (yes, *that* profession), and for almost her entire life, she was an outlaw.

If you've ever doubted one person's ability to rule her own empire, let me introduce you to Ching Shih, *the* most successful pirate in history. If you thought Blackbeard or Redbeard (or even the mythological Captain Jack Sparrow) was a force of infamous and swashbuckling heroism, just wait until you hear about Ching Shih.

Like many legendary human beings, less is written about her than historians would like. What has been written has been contradicted. What has been passed down is often exaggerated, or, conversely, underreported. The truth lies somewhere in the midst of all the rumors. I'll share the research, and let you decide what's true. But there is one fact many pirate enthusiasts and historians agree on: No pirate in history was as successful, culturally or economically, as Ching Shih.

In the early 1800s, under the waning power of the Chinese Qing dynasty, piracy was alive and well. Likely to attract visitors to their ports, the minorities within the Canton region (modern Guangzhou) had a unique offering called "flower boats." On these ornately decorated boats, young ladies would meander from ship to ship, offering services to the young sailors, such as dancing, companionship, and sometimes intimacy.

Here, as a flower-boat girl, Ching Shih found her first career success. She was smart, interesting, and, of course, beautiful. By some records, her reputation had put her in high demand among the other young ladies, and she ultimately claimed many high-profile pirates, politicians, and businessmen as her regular clients. Because of her clientele, she'd hear rumors, gossip, and inside dealings. She had as much blackmail fodder as she did beauty.

One of her clients, a pirate captain named Zheng Yi, was the leader of the well-known and feared Red Flag Fleet. Infatuated with Ching Shih, one evening he ordered his men to kidnap her. They tied her up and brought her to him. When she arrived, he asked if she'd like to marry him. The henchmen untied her so she could give her answer—*bad call.*

As the story goes, "When she was untied in order to give her answer, she sprang at him like a banshee and attempted to claw his eyes out."[1] (I guess none of the pirates had read *Getting to Yes* at this point in their careers.)

Nonetheless, Ching Shih and Zheng Yi negotiated. She agreed to marry him under the condition that she would own half of all his fleet. Amazingly, he agreed, and the two quickly became the Bonnie and Clyde of the high seas. Zheng Yi came from a long line of ruthless pirates. Ching Shih had blackmail and other critical information on many of the most powerful people in the known world. Under their combined leadership, they organized the entire pirating community into a strict, hierarchical structure. Ching Shih believed that by working together instead of constantly having "turf wars," the pirates could all enjoy more wealth. They rallied the entire pirating underworld—some 50,000 pirates and hundreds of vessels—under a confederation of about a half-dozen pirate leaders, organizing them into territories, assigning rank, and having each report upward, ultimately to Ching Shih and Zheng Yi.

If you've seen *Pirates of the Caribbean 3*, then you may remember a character, Mistress Ching, sitting at the table of the nine Pirate Lords. Many speculate that the writers of the film modeled her after Ching Shih. But even that's not giving her enough credit. The truth is, the entire concept—of a roundtable of rule-abiding pirate leaders—is owed, at least in part, to Ching Shih.[2] One of her lasting pirate legacies is the enforcement of a code. Perhaps influenced by her upbringing, she enforced a strict set of rules in her private kingdom: no stealing, desertion, or rape. Women were to be treated with respect at all times.

After her husband passed, Ching Shih not only seized the helm of the pirate confederation but expanded it. The desperate Chinese government tried everything; yet Ching Shih's military prowess and organizational skills allowed her to not only evade capture, but continually defeat armada after armada from the Chinese government. Ultimately the government asked for help from the Dutch, the British, and the Portuguese. Everyone tried—everyone failed.

At her height, Ching Shih commanded 1,800 large ships and smaller vessels—more than the modern navies of the United States, China, Russia, and Japan . . . *combined.* She also ran an empire of up to 80,000 men.[3] By comparison, Meta (formerly Facebook) had about 77,000 employees in 2022.

Perhaps the greatest part of Ching Shih's legacy is that she recognized that the pirates—known for disorderly conduct and inbred fighting—needed organization and unity. For tyrants who steal and kill for a living, formal organization is a disruptive paradigm. By sensing the need and executing on it, Ching Shih capitalized on her moment, seizing an opportunity that others had been unable to capture. There was a harvest of opportunity available, and it took an inexperienced pirate to take the real treasure.

Being bold enough to create a hierarchy and a code (the very things pirates hated) required an individual like Ching Shih, who was a bloodthirsty, fearless tyrant.

Now fast-forward about 200 years, and leave the waters of the high seas for the garments of fashion. In the 2010s, the beauty and intimate apparel industries had problems as obvious as those of the nineteenth-century Chinese pirates, and again it needed a Bold One to disrupt them both. So in 2017, in walked another heroine from across the seas, this time from Barbados:

Rihanna.

Rihanna, having already taken the music industry by storm, set her sights on the beauty industry. For years, it had been plagued by an ineptitude to create colors, tones, and makeup for anyone but light-skinned women. Particularly among minorities, the problem was obvious.

True, a few notable, niche companies served their respective communities, but "Rihanna" *wasn't* a small name. And she wasn't about to settle for anything less than the whole fleet.

Her first major collaboration was with LVMH—the most prolific luxury brand in the world. Rihanna didn't just make a small handful of diversity-friendly tones; instead, she filled a kaleidoscope with *40* different shades. She released her Beauty Fenty line with LVMH, and within 40 days, the line had sold $100 million in product.

But Rihanna wasn't done.

She set her sights on the intimate apparel industry, where exactly one tall, white giant had ruled for decades, Victoria's Secret.

Rihanna aimed her cannons right at their mast—the lingerie runway show.

Rihanna unashamedly took their own models, poaching six Victoria's Secret "angels" and renaming them "savages." Then she collaborated with Amazon—the dirty dog of retail—to host her own catwalk show, one that celebrated women of all colors and all sizes. Unlike its competition, Rihanna's show highlighted mostly female acts, and all the marketing—from the choreography of the dancers to the diversity of the models—was aimed at the desires of women, not the eyes of men.

Within a year of Rihanna's Savage Fenty show, Victoria's Secret—a 44-year-old company—had lost sales, its stock was sinking, and its runway shows were canceled; then, in 2021, its parent company announced they'd be spinning the brand off into its own company. That's the power of being bold.

In 1800, everyone knew that the underworld needed order.

In 2000, everyone knew the world of underwear needed disruption.

In both cases, it took a Bold One to rewrite history.

CREATE A CULT

Let's begin this section by defining the word *cult*. A cult is a small, rugged offshoot of a larger system. A cult breaks off the mainstream, going rogue before it ever becomes popular and attracts the masses.

In one of his most famous quotes, renowned science fiction writer L. Ron Hubbard, the author of *Battlefield Earth*, once supposedly said, "You don't get rich writing science fiction. If you want to get rich, you start a *religion*."[4, 5]

Hubbard, who also founded the religion Scientology, was casting light on something even more profound than the relationship between finances and religion. He was showing that if you really want to influence people, you've got to create a following so intense, so dedicated, that in the end you don't just have an audience who's following a brand. To influence the world, you need a cult.

This might sound extreme, but hang with me. Think of the most influential brand names and properties in the world—the ones that constantly attract outsized attention from the media, top talent, and partners. Immediately, you'll notice two things.

One, it's not usually the company, but one person, such as the founder or an individual creator, who's attracted all the attention. When you think about Apple, you think of Steve Jobs. When you think about Harry Potter, you think of J. K. Rowling. When you think about Microsoft, Tesla, or Disney, you think, respectively, about Bill Gates, Elon Musk, or Walt Disney. In many cases, we don't even think about the company at all; more people are familiar with Warren Buffet than with his company, Berkshire Hathaway. People are more likely to recognize Oprah than her production company, Harpo Productions.

In a sense, these individuals have become mini-religions.

The second thing you'll notice about the most iconic brand names in the world is the level of intimacy that these founders sometimes inspire among their followers. For instance, when Steve Jobs passed away, Apple created a permanent scrolling feed for Steve Jobs's idolizers to post their feelings:

"His legacy will be eternal."—Gabriel
"Today we lost a visionary genius."—Mary
"A true human hero."—Hugh

Eternal. Visionary. Hero. Those aren't words you'd typically leave on a feedback form after visiting an electronics store to pick up a laptop. Those are the kinds of things people say when an icon has passed.

For something truly disruptive—such as a new product, a revolutionized platform, or a creative method of accomplishing an outcome—we're eventually going to need a dedicated following—a devout group of individuals who turn into employees, evangelists, and partners.

How do we do that? How do we build a following that dedicated? How do we become the pirate captain of our own fleet and create a cultlike following that will come behind us as we break down the walls of the institutions? There are five steps we can learn from our two pirate heroes and other leaders:

> **STEP 1: INSPIRE THE UNDERDOGS.** Notice how Ching Shih and Rihanna didn't go after the main cohorts and demographics of their marketplaces? Instead, they inspired loyalty among those who'd been marginalized by others.
> **STEP 2: CREATE A HALO EFFECT.** It's possible to do something so revolutionary and awe-inspiring that whatever

you do *next* will have the touch of the gods. Rihanna can start any business she wants—she goes from music to lingerie to skin care—because to her followers, she walks on water.

STEP 3: CAPITALIZE ON FRACTURED MEDIA. You actually have an *advantage* over Ching Shih. It's easier now, more than ever, to reach a niche following. The world has splintered, and as a result has created an endless number of channels for leaders and followers to connect over unique interests, passions, and ideas. You can utilize these channels to reach a small but dedicated fan base.

STEP 4: UNDERSTAND THE PARADOX OF PIRACY. You must keep in mind what I call the "paradox of piracy," a seeming contradiction that suggests if you want to go broad in the long run, you've got to start by thinking niche in the short run.

STEP 5: AVOID THE DARK SIDE OF THE CULT. What happens when you build walls so high on your status that they create an echo chamber, one where no one dares challenge you? The better job you do at creating a cultlike following, the harder it will be to disrupt yourself. Be on guard against the dark side of the cult.

Let's dive deeper into each of these key concepts.

STEP 1. INSPIRE THE UNDERDOGS

Typically, a cult attracts the underdogs, those that everyone else has overlooked. While 90 percent of the world looks at the same cohorts, demographics, and geographies, Bold Ones think differently.

Victoria's Secret maintained its domination for a long time by doubling down on exactly one body type. The company even knowingly ostracized others; as their CMO Ed Razek infamously remarked to *Vogue,* "I don't think we can be all things to all customers." However insensitive, Razek's comment made sense in old-school thinking: optimization for the greatest ROI. Wielding its monopolistic stranglehold on the industry, the company had little reason to negotiate with fringe needs. Before 2018, if you wanted luxury lingerie, you shopped at Victoria's Secret. That was *the* option. But Bold Ones think differently. They look internally and consider their own authentic voice, culture, and experiences. They recognize they don't have to compete for that singular, sought-after demographic. Instead, they can remain true to a central group of people to defeat institutionalized incumbents. They can create their own cultlike following from a dedicated, small group of believers who are willing to sail with them into uncharted waters. While institutions always look down on these fringes, Bold Ones embrace them.

When others are looking to hire from Ivy League institutions, Bold Ones ask where the untapped potential is in the warehouses. While incumbents chase the same celebrities, geographies, and talent, Bold Ones are looking to get out of the mainstream and into the less-crowded, overlooked areas of society.

One of the greatest heroes in Jewish culture is King David—you know, the one we all talk about in the David versus Goliath story. But there's a lot more to his story than a towering giant and a slingshot-wielding underdog.

Before David became king, he was actually an outlaw to his own people. The king at the time, Saul, wanted to *kill* David out of jealousy. So David ran off to hide in the middle of the mountains. That actually became his setup.

While up there in the crags, he started making friends. Not friends from the nice nobility of the palace, but criminals, outcasts, and lonely people. Even foreigners—a big no-no in Jewish culture of that day—became his closest friends. David started to create an unexpected and loyal following.

David eventually overcame his outlaw status and became king of Israel, and what people did he bring with him? That band of brothers. They become his elite fighting force.

Here's the thing about niche crowds: When you befriend them, they're fiercely loyal. Once, during a war, King David complained that he didn't have any fresh water. Do you know what the elite men in his army did? Attacked another *kingdom*, just to get clean, fresh water for David.

That's loyalty. That's the kind of emotional connection you breed when you root for the underdogs.

You can do the same by looking for a niche cohort in forgotten areas: in a talent pool, in an underserved market, or in a disaffected geography. Ching Shih embraced the outlaws; Rihanna embraced multiple skin tones. Whom or what can you embrace? While everyone else is distracted by the majority, those on the fringe, forgotten and lonely, are ready to be awakened. Plus, there are fewer gatekeepers, less rules, and usually no competition.

So how do you embrace the underdogs?

I have four suggestions, starting with your audience.

BE CLEAR ON YOUR AUDIENCE

Create your offerings or content with target personas in mind. Building a community of supporters that grows with you is one of the hardest things to do, so you want to get this right.

If you're trying to inspire the underdogs, be *clear* about who those underdogs are, specifically. When you're building out content, creating products, or taking a stand on an issue, make sure everything is aligned to attract those you're trying to inspire.

In his book *Content-Based Networking,* author James Carbary says it like this: "Work *backward* from the exact goals you have in mind, from the place you want to *end up,* [and] the connections that you need."

One of the *best* connections that you can make? A connection with the "number two" person in an organization.

LOOK FOR THE NUMBER TWO

Malcolm Gladwell, the famous author and thinker (another Canadian!) talks about learning from the number two person, not the head leader. Everyone wants to speak with the CEO of a company or the president of a nation. But while the top dogs have inundated inboxes, the number two person within each organization is just waiting for the chance to share *their* story.

Not only are you more likely to get a response from someone in this position, but Gladwell points out that you're actually more likely to get the real truth from these individuals as well, because they aren't constantly filtering everything through a list of PR-whitewashed filters; the number twos—like the executive assistant, campaign manager, or vice president—are more likely to be bold, unafraid, and willing to share their real thoughts. So, as you're building out your cultlike following, don't get distracted by the celebrities or the demographics stealing 99 percent of the world's attention.

CONNECT AND COLLABORATE

Collaborations are essential for growth. Essentially, look for an opportunity to work *with others* in a real way, even for free. This could be a small project, a piece of content, a new podcast, or a mini-project. Is there a side project you can take on at work?

Can you build a piece of content with others that allows you to build out your network? Remember, you don't always need to be captaining the ship.

TRUST ISN'T BUILT OVERNIGHT

When you're first building your fleet of influence, you'll need patience. Focus on delivering ridiculously high-quality, meaningful offerings to your audience or team members. If you're in a position to hire team members, give them ample opportunity to pursue their favorite projects. If you decide to build out a YouTube channel for your audience, forget making money, and instead ask yourself, "What does my audience need that I can provide?" If the people in your audience need to hear from an expert, find experts for your show. If they need real-world examples, offer them. If they need a template, hop on Google Docs and build one.

If you're consistent with delivering value, your audience, teammates, and partners will reward you. I've been posting a video every week on LinkedIn for almost four years. It took some time to get any real traction; now I have thousands of followers across my platforms. Build the habit, and focus on value.

STEP 2. CREATE A HALO EFFECT

Creating a cultlike audience that will follow you into the depths can be difficult, but there is a trick—a hack, if you will—that you can use to do something disruptive. Similar to the 3% Rule, this one is a time-tested tactic that's simple to copy.

It's called the "halo effect." Originally coined by one of the most prolific and cited psychologists of the 1900s, Edward

Thorndike,[6] a halo effect occurs when you do something so spectacular that, by association, anything else you do has a ring of angelic grace to it. With the halo effect, once you've executed in one area with awe-inspiring diligence, your community now views everything you do with anticipation and, likely, appreciation. There are lots of example of how this works, but my favorite is Kanye West and Adidas.

The controversial rapper, self-proclaimed fashionista, and one-time US presidential candidate got fed up with the shoe company he was repping, Nike. So he dropped them, and in 2013, he walked a couple of blocks over to a competitor, Adidas.

In the early 2010s, the Adidas brand was stagnating, while others, particularly Nike, were gaining market share. Always a rebel, Kanye didn't want to be a simple brand ambassador for Adidas. He wanted to take the company into a whole new niche: lifestyle sneakers. It wasn't something Adidas was known for, but they gave Kanye the go-ahead, and a new collaboration was born: "Yeezy."

It was a hit.

Kanye's Midas touch gave the entire company a brand lift, ushering in a new breed of consumers, and the entire Adidas brand enjoyed a resurgence in popularity. At the time of writing this book, Kanye's relationship with Adidas has been strained—that's a whole another story!

Kanye took his own halo, built on his fan base from music, and applied it to an entirely new product. Fans liked Kanye, so they liked Yeezy: halo effect. Adidas was thrilled:

Not only [have the Yeezy's] sold out instantly, but [they've] also played a major role in propelling Adidas to the most popular sneaker brand on Instagram in 2015.[7]

How can you apply a halo effect to your own career and personal brand? What's something you can create that's stand-alone enough, unique enough, and authentic enough to you, that it casts an angelic light over everything you do, one that will follow you as you keep pushing for disruption? Say you're a real estate mogul who's into racing electric vehicles as a hobby; why not start a blog about it? It's low-investment, you enjoy it, and if you can become an expert in one area, it gives you the appearance of expertise in all areas.

Perhaps my favorite example of a halo effect comes from two French brothers, Édouard and André.

In the early 1900s, the brothers owned a tire company. In an attempt to generate more sales, they created a world-class restaurant rating book, called the *Michelin Guide*. Originally, they thought they could push more people to drive farther distances, thereby increasing the demand for new tires. However, the guide quickly became so well respected in the restaurant industry, that its real power is that the name "Michelin" now stands for world-class quality in two areas: top-rated restaurants and excellent car tires.

BUILD A PERSONAL MOAT

Medieval rulers defended their positions by placing moats around their castles. Today, a personal moat around your own brand allows you to possess something that's so uniquely your own, it's essentially a personal monopoly.

There are myriad ways to build a personal moat. You can combine various skills (like law and cryptocurrency), layer in locality on top of your expertise (like "the best real estate agent in Sedona, Arizona"), or just be the only expert in your field who's also a black belt in karate.

Take Kiersten and Julien Saunders, personal finance experts who also have a passion for cooking. They created an entire WebTV series called *Money on the Table*, where they bring financial conversation to their own kitchen table as they cook a meal. With that, they've created a unique personal brand; and in 2021, a major studio contacted them to start recording their first "real" TV episode. Then, in 2022, they dropped their own book, *Cashing Out*. Who can compete with fantastic cooks who also know everything there is to know about finances?

I've tried to add this personal moat into my own life. At my keynotes, I speak about disruption. By itself, that's not much of a differentiator. However, I've raised a flag around my brand by combining pop culture with disruption. While others focus on technological disruptors, I use references that are part of the cultural zeitgeist. Using a strategy commonly referred to as "newsjacking," I'll grab a current event and connect it with a broader idea.

Look hard enough, and it's not difficult to understand your own style, and that's your differentiator. You may be a nurse practitioner, and, sure, there are lots of nurse practitioners. But few of them are likely to care about the same sports teams as you do. Perhaps you're a software developer, and you have a lot of competition. But do your colleagues know that you also double as a comedian? (Scott Adams, a developer, found a new core when he became the author of the renowned comic strip *Dilbert*.) Perhaps you're one of a thousand auditors in your Big Four auditing firm where most want to work the biggest-name clients; does everyone know that you love working with the smaller clients?

Ultimately you want to find something that is portable and tactical and that only you are known for. You want to associate yourself with a specific artifact—whether a niche type of content, a specific community, or a particular skill set—that others can point to and say, "Ah, that's their thing."

Start building out your authentic personal moat, and make your castle unique.

IF ALL ELSE FAILS . . .

There's a story someone on my media team told me about his friend, Brandon, who's now a voice actor working on video games.

He got into the highly competitive industry by starting at Disney World. With no prior knowledge of the industry, no real hard skills, and no experience, he took a high school acting class and told his teacher he wanted to audition for Disney. The teacher gave him one single piece of advice:

Make sure they remember you.

He used the example of someone who was trying out for the male lead in *Romeo and Juliet*. Likely, dozens (if not hundreds) of men wanted the part, and they had all memorized the audition scene to perfection. But then, one man did something the casting director couldn't forget—he climbed up the curtains to reach for an invisible Juliet as he read his lines.

Guess who got the part?

If you can't quite think of how to differentiate yourself, lean on your quirks, interests, and those things about you no one else does quite like you, even if they aren't directly related to your expertise. If all else fails, *make sure they remember you.*

STEP 3. CAPITALIZE ON FRACTURED MEDIA

Reaching a lonely, ostracized community has become easier as technology has shifted. While working on the flower boats, Ching Shih had to spend time with each individual to extract knowledge she'd need to leverage later: one hour of time for one hour of information. But now? You can scale her efforts in a way never possible before. You can double down on Ching Shih's genius, even without her singular personality or rare opportunities.

With social media, people from the other side of the globe can get in your head. They can hear your thoughts on politics, business, and socioeconomics by following you on social media. You can feature your art on Patreon, allowing fans to support you financial. With the revolution of direct-to-consumer sales, you can be a pirate in your world, a one-person show. Whatever niche community of people you are attempting to reach, you can find them at the click of a button.

Plus, we don't all have to buy into one common narrative anymore. We have multiple options of what to consume, believe, and understand.

Previously, certain gatekeepers told society what to think, how to act, and when to buy. For much of history, advertising, media, education, and other distributors of information created a familiar few narratives from which followers were allowed to choose. For centuries, the Catholic Church dictated when you could work, how you could perform medicine, and whom you could marry. Before the church, there was the Roman Empire. Before the empire, there were the Egyptian pharaohs. While a few notable individuals broke through these institutionalized boundaries, the gates were high.

Today the smartphone has become the new church. It dictates every aspect of our lives. The difference between the old churches and this new church is that the new church is hyper customized to the individual. Attention has been fractured into a billion pieces, and the smartphone has become a portal for us to engage with anyone all over the world.

I worship Bill Simmons. I wait every Sunday evening for the new Bill Simmons piece to hear his takes on the NBA and pop culture. I've never talked to or met Bill Simmons in my life, but I've listened to more than a thousand of his hour-long podcasts. I hate to admit this (and I'm sure Bill Simmons would hate to admit this too), but because of the phone, I am part of the Bill Simmons cult.

Look at Joe Rogan, the Kardashians, Alexandria Ocasio-Cortez, Steve Jobs, Jordan Peterson, or Donald Trump. All of them have inspired cultlike followings purely through a screen. Their political leanings are conflicting, and their fields are varied; yet all of them have reached those who are willing to argue, fight, and lose friends over their causes. Extreme? Yes. Effective? Absolutely.

In our case, we can leave the controversy and still capitalize on the fragmentation. This new wave of diversified media provides a global audience, making mass connection possible through just one device. You can exercise your influence over a niche, but expand that influence across the globe. A Bold One could not only learn, but master, infiltrate, and completely derail the course of an industry from the confines of home. While we used to hear "Every company is its own media company," now we can also say "Every *person* is their own media company."

You and I must capitalize on this opportunity and begin to inspire our teams or followers.

To capitalize on this fragmentation, you need to build a unique advantage around your personality. Next you also need to find the right medium for that personality, the right channel that can carry information.

FIND THE PERFECT MEDIUM

Once you've started creating your own personal brand, you must display it on a medium that can garner attention, one that fits well with your information and your community.

Whether it's video, audio, writing, events, text messages, or group chats, place your ideas on a platform that has the ability to reach one more person. Find the medium that best suits your personality and skills. One more supporter tomorrow is two more supporters next month, and four the month after that.

"SHIP" IT

Since we're on pirates, let's talk about the word "ship" for a moment. This is where a lot of people get it wrong. They don't ship their content. They don't click the "send," "upload," or "post" button. They do all the work but never publish that content, or send the email to the connection they want to make, or show up at the coffee shop to meet with the new potential partner. When you're building an audience, a fan base, connections, coworkers, or content, you need to go for it. Get a little uncomfortable, and start making moves.

STEP 4. UNDERSTAND THE PARADOX OF PIRACY

When bold pirates are willing to inspire the underdogs, capitalize on fractured media, and create their own halo, they discover what I call the "paradox of piracy."

It's a seeming contradiction, but it's a simple premise: When you aim for a fringe, you ultimately attract the masses.

You can start a radical journey on a flower boat, but end up as the captain of the world's largest naval confederation. When you create a following so deep, so devout via your own authenticity, ignoring whatever is considered "the masses" to devote yourself to the few, you're able to create something so worthwhile, everyone wants to jump on board.

Rihanna's success with fringe skin tones parlayed into a broader culture. In 2019, when the luxury lingerie brand announced it was canceling its renowned fashion show, Rihanna did her first. While Victoria's Secret announced it was closing nearly 250 locations in 2020, Savage X took its first dive into physical stores. "Savage X doesn't hold any punches, and it's all gas, no brakes," Rihanna said in an interview with *Refinery 29*.[8]

For a while, major institutions—such as banks, Fortune 100 businesses, and universities—had all the power. Much like their concrete structures, their influences were cemented into our hearts and minds—their power towered over our ambitions, casting shadows everywhere.

But people would rather follow Anderson Cooper over CNN. In sports, people often cheer for their favorite players, regardless of what jersey they wear.

People more devoutly follow *individuals*, not brands. Humans want to be part of what's bigger than themselves: a movement, an ideology, something that has meaning and purpose.

You can start small, with your niche audience; but in the end, the reward is, you capture the attention of the masses. If you want to change the game, start with one piece. If you want to disrupt an incumbent, look for a fringe group that was missed. If you want to upset an industry, go find one fan, and deliver insane value to them.

That's the paradox of piracy.

STEP 5. AVOID THE DARK SIDE OF THE CULT

To achieve disruption, you'll need devotion and resilience from a fearless group. The only way to achieve massive disruption is to think fringe, first.

The beauty of such a following is evident, but there's a dark side of creating such a fan base. Eventually, you could gain so much attention and success, that you'll wrestle with what every incumbent institution faces—having to break out of the high walls you've built around yourself. Boldness is easier when you have nothing to lose.

If your dedicated audience expects you to act one way, what if you behave in another? If you built your reputation on the back of a hard stance on remote work, what will "they" say when your opinion shifts?

Social media makes this even more challenging. The more you lean to a particular side, the more attention you receive. The algorithms push the most outlandish ideas because that's what generates the most engagement. I've seen the algorithms turn thought leaders into caricatures of themselves.

Breaking out of a mold you've created can be challenging, but it can be done.

Consider Howard Stern. I've listened to the self-proclaimed "King of All Media" since 2007, and I can tell you that he's changed in both tone and substance. Originally he was brash, unapologetic, and provocative. He gained an audience with his unique style. Over time, he's toned that all down significantly. Plus, his political views have drastically changed. In today's world, those aren't easy swings to make. But with a willingness to evolve, you can constantly disrupt yourself, and avoid being disrupted by an external force.

I have one piece of advice that will help ensure you never succumb to the seductive pull of success or algorithms:

Create your own advisory team.

The greater your status, the less likely fans will guide you when you're off track. They won't feel the need—or ability—to speak up. That's why you need to intentionally surround yourself with people who will call you out.

Create a fearless advisory team who don't get mesmerized with status. Empower them to challenge you. This doesn't have to be complicated. You just need a group of tight individuals whom you trust to give you honest feedback. Personally, I have a WhatsApp group—ironically called "Kardashians"—with some of my absolute closest friends. I use it for my brain dumps, ideas, and vulnerabilities. If any one in the group makes a comment about my tone or substance, I immediately listen. I don't want to build an echo chamber. I want outside influence, and a broad view of the world. Go get your own advisory team together.

EVEN PIRATES RETIRE

Ching Shih faced the dark side of the cult at one point in her career—she'd outmaneuvered much of the globe's Eastern empires. She'd outcommanded their navies and outpirated the greatest buccaneers of her day. But pirating can only last so long. When she decided to disrupt her current career, to retire, she couldn't exactly settle down to a normal life with a 401(k) and a beach house in the Florida Keys. In perhaps a stunning pivot, Ching Shih decided to negotiate her surrender in 1810.

This move was one of her boldest yet—no guns, no men, just an appeal to the Qing government. She marched up to the governor's house, armed with nothing more than other women and children, to boldly negotiate, face-to-face, with the enemy. She offered to stop all piracy, under the condition that none of her fleet's stolen goods would be returned. She also demanded that the Chinese government not only pay her, but pay the men under her as well.

The government accepted the terms.

One woman united the entire underworld and routed China for years, escaping every known navy on earth. And then she died peacefully in her own home.

Even while creating a cult, she kept the longest view in the ocean. While she was enjoying success on the open seas, she knew it wouldn't last. She allowed herself to evolve, even past her own successes. Many may have thought that she'd drifted so far out into the ocean of treachery, she could never return to normality. But she proved them all wrong.

She was willing to disrupt herself, even to the end. That's the final lesson we can learn from Ching Shih: Never stop disrupting yourself, because even pirates can retire.

SECRETS OF THE BOLD ONES

INSPIRE THE UNDERDOGS. The deepest loyalties are on the fringes. Religious cults always start out this way, preaching to those who feel marginalized. Do likewise: Find the cohort, the fringe group, the geography that the incumbents are forgetting about. Build your community there.

CREATE A HALO EFFECT. A halo effect occurs when you build something deep and authentic around your personality. This could be an asset, a piece of technology, or an idea. Get known for it, and deliver it. If all else fails, make sure people remember you.

CAPITALIZE ON FRACTURED MEDIA. You have something the pirates of old never had; you can capitalize on the fact that there are less gatekeepers than ever. Fewer institutions are holding the keys, and there are endless channels you can use to reach your ideal audience. You only need one to win.

UNDERSTAND THE PARADOX OF PIRACY. When you shoot for the niches, you ultimately inspire the crowds. Incumbents have it wrong. They try to protect what they've already won, and this leaves them vulnerable to you, as you can circle the fringes to penetrate a way into the masses.

AVOID THE DARK SIDE OF THE CULT. When you create a profound following, you can build deep wells—grooves—that ultimately blind you to your own errors or vulnerabilities. To ensure you're always open to evolution, create an advisory team of select individuals whom you empower to challenge you and your ideas directly.

CHAPTER 5

DISRUPTION IS A JOKE

First they ignore you, then they laugh at
you, then they fight you, then you win.
—MAHATMA GANDHI[1]

He's been called "The Greatest Business Tycoon of India,"
"The Man Who Saw Tomorrow," and "The Father of Indian
Industrialization."

By the numbers, he's the world's single greatest philanthropist,
having given to others more than the next three contestants—Bill
Gates, Warren Buffett, and George Soros—*combined*. He founded
one of the world's grandest lodgings, the Taj Mahal Hotel. His
foresight allowed India to become Britain's main importer of cotton, overtaking America as the world's leading cotton distributor,
when he started an Indian entrepreneurial uprising, right under
the nose of the British occupation.

He traveled the world to commandeer the greatest inventors and invite them to his home country, convinced the entire cotton industry to move thousands of miles away from the ports, instituted novel human resources benefits (like retirement and medical plans) for his employees, and was present at the 1885 Indian National Congress.

His name was Jamsetji Tata, and his résumé reads like an Indian version of Henry Ford's and George Washington's put together.

The family name "Tata" is the Indian equivalent of the Rockefellers. Tata Industries owns companies in almost every category imaginable, from airlines to automobiles, from chemicals to communications, and from Starbucks partnerships to sports teams.

This all resulted from the Tata patriarch, and our next Bold One, Jamsetji.[2]

With no deep pedigreed family name to speak of, no trust fund, and no training, Jamsetji rose from working in a small, almost nonexistent family business, to founding one that upset the world's economy.

If you want to understand Jamsetji, know this: From his poor upbringing through his eventual richest-man-in-the-country status, he remained a man of the world, traveling to as many countries as he could. China, Canada, the United States, Great Britain, Hong Kong, Syria, Morocco, Egypt, Russia, France . . . the list goes on. To understand this innovator, you've got to travel with him. So let's head to Hong Kong, 1859.

His father had a small opium outfit in India, and he sent Jamsetji overseas to better understand their relationship with their Chinese business partners. While there, Jamsetji discovered something far more profitable than opium: cotton. His disruptive hunch told him this would become the economic game changer his home country needed. He returned home with an untested but passionate theory: Indians could revolutionize their own cotton production and distribute it across the globe, thereby loosening the economic stranglehold of the British, who were occupying India.

If British occupation had taught him anything, it was that the West was willing to pay for what it wanted. India had the homegrown population necessary for a vibrant workforce, the ports required for global distribution, and plenty of land (used mostly for opium) to grow cotton. India was set up to be the cotton king of the world. The country just needed to wiggle out from under the British thumb.

Perhaps as the "pilot" to his future endeavors, Jamsetji purchased a bankrupt Indian mill, which he turned around and sold for a profit within two years.

Game on.

By then, Bombay was producing a sizable minority of the known world's cotton, and due to its location on the west coast of India, had easy access to well-established ports for international distribution. There were already 15 mills running in Bombay. To most, this was the obvious city to headquarter a renegade cotton empire. But Jamsetji saw it differently. He wanted to set up his new business venture thousands of kilometers *inland*, away from the ports, in Nagpur. His counterparts scoffed—it would take four months just for the arrival of the needed equipment—which would have to come from the West, travel to an Indian port, then be pulled by bullocks (by oxcart) all the way to Nagpur. "What a bad idea," I can almost imagine them saying to themselves under their breath.

But Jamsetji was relentless, and his inland Empress Mill was born. It became one of the most profitable companies in the country, laying the foundation of the iconic Tata Group, according to Think School,[3] which goes on to say one of my favorite lines about Jamsetji: "Even then, Jamsetji didn't stop."

He launched a successful iron company and set up a world-class science- and technology-based Indian university, all of which helped India claim financial liberation from the grip of colonial Britain. He also started the Taj Mahal Hotel. Legend has it he was denied entry to a fancy Indian lodging, *because* he was Indian, not British. So he decided he'd build one of the world's greatest hotels for his own people. And he did.

Get what was going on? Here was some Indian upstart who had some unrealistic, optimistic belief in his ability to just start his own company, without appeasing the British powers that be. Then he moved his mill *away* from the ports. Every move this guy made seemed ridiculous.

To the occupying British, I imagine Jamsetji's ideas probably sounded like one big joke. What they didn't know? They were the punchline.

Jamsetji's impact can be summarized by what Lord Curzon, the British viceroy of India, said about him when he passed:

No Indian of the present generation had done more for the commerce and industry of India.

IT'S A JOKE (UNTIL IT'S NOT)

Disruption always begins as hilarious, fringe, and, sometimes, almost pathetic. I remember going over to my friend Ryan's house when I was younger. In those days, only the really blessed kids had four controllers. Most (if they were even lucky enough to have a console) had one controller, or *maybe* two. Ryan wasn't one of the super-blessed kids, and he hadn't exactly learned about sharing yet. So I'd tell my mom, "Hey, Mom. I'm going to Ryan's house to watch him play video games." I was trying to be funny, but watching someone play video games was almost depressing. It was better than doing chores, but it still made me want to scream "When is it *my* turn?!"

If you'd have told young Shawn that one day there would be an entire company dedicated to streaming video games so others could watch, I'd have laughed. If you'd have told me that not only would that company exist, but it would be worth billions, I would have thought you were certifiable. But, Twitch is a platform designed so that people can tune in and watch other people play video games. In 2014, Amazon bought the platform for almost $1 billion,[4] and it now has 140 million daily active users.[5]

Disruption always starts out as some seemingly silly idea. Most people miss the wave, because it was disguised as laughable. Think about automobiles, SMS messaging, Airbnb, or Creators. Someone, somewhere—maybe even you—resisted:

AUTOMOBILES. "These 'auto-carriages' are slower than my horse!"

SMS MESSAGING. "Why would people text when they could call?"

AIRBNB. "Right—so people will just show up at a stranger's home and *live* there?"

CREATORS. "You videotape yourself in your bedroom, and post it for strangers to watch?"

All these comments have some logical merit. But who's laughing now? Disruptors see the future and bring it into the present. Others think, *Is this person crazy?* But it's not the disruptor who's crazy—it's everyone else who passes on the investment, misses the wave, or doesn't comprehend what's happening around them.

Somehow we've made it cool to be openly cynical. We think we appear smarter when we're reflexively dismissive of new, disruptive ideas.

There's a clip I like to show in many of my speeches; it's a 1995 scene with David Letterman and Bill Gates. They're discussing the internet, a novel technology few understood at the time. Letterman—and almost everyone else alive in 1995—didn't get why it was going to be such a big deal. Letterman said that others had mentioned that the internet would be useful because it could help you broadcast a baseball game. To that, Letterman had an easy comeback:

"Does *radio* ring a bell?" he said. The audience laughed hysterically.

"But," Gates noted, "you can listen to the baseball game whenever you want."

"Do *tape recorders* ring a bell?" Letterman shot back.

Anytime people dismiss what they see as silly, they're set up to be the punchline of their own joke.

In the rest of the chapter, we're going to determine how *we* can have the last laugh. Here's what you need to know:

1. **ONLY CONTRARIANS WIN BIG.** Even if we're right, conforming to society or common thought processes drives little (if any) real value, and certainly no true innovation. To drive the most value, you must go against the crowd *and*, simultaneously, be right in your contrarian ideas.

2. **IT ONLY TAKES ONE HIT.** You might be wrong a lot more than you're right. But the one time you're right will pay off big. You need to swing at the ball, often and fiercely, in order to get a hit.

3. **YOU'LL HAVE THE LAST LAUGH.** Typically, we're far too worried about what others think about us. So, we fail to keep our eye on the prize that we know is worth fighting for. We must learn how to let the opinions of others roll off our backs.

If we're going to be disruptive, we've got to keep a thick skin, and trust me, it's so worth a few laughs here and there. Because in the fringes, the silly ideas, the contrarian outlooks, have all the value.

ONLY CONTRARIANS WIN BIG

Peter Weinberg, global head of development at LinkedIn's B2B Institute, talks about the Contrarian Matrix, a matrix he divides into four quadrants dependent on two variables: (1) You can be either right or wrong about where the world's going, and (2) regardless of whether you're correct or not, you can either go with the consensus or be a contrarian.[6] Figure 5.1 shows how the Contrarian Matrix breaks down.

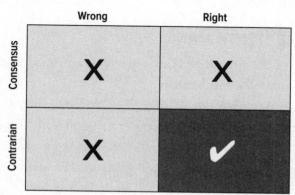

FIGURE 5.1 The Contrarian Matrix

Notice the checkmark in the box at the bottom right? That's because Weinberg says that's the only quadrant that holds any value.

If you're wrong and you go with the consensus, no one cares, because the whole world was wrong. You're safe—wrong, but safe.

If you're right and go with the consensus, you gain a little, but you miss out on huge gains; follow general stock market advice, and you'll make an 8 percent return on average.

If you're wrong and contrarian, people will laugh. That's a real bummer, because not only will people get the first laugh, but you'll never get the last. (We'll talk more about how to deal with this later.)

Only by being both *right* and *contrarian* can you change the game and discover untapped value. If you bet against the market and you're right, you'll earn 10 times your investment. If all the others pass on an employee because they don't recognize their unique gifts, you stand to mine unrealized potential. If all the others get a degree in technology, but you go into art, you'll be one of a few artists who can corner the market, commanding high prices.

I think there are three ways to be the contrarian.

1. BE THE "TENTH MAN"

This idea of the contrarian is so important, an entire *country* uses it as a self-defense mechanism.

While watching *World War Z* with Brad Pitt, audiences around the globe learned about Israel's supposed "Tenth Man Rule." Analysts have debated whether this is an official policy of the real State of Israel, but regardless, the lesson remains. Supposedly, after the 1973 Yom Kippur War (where Egypt and

Syria launched a surprise attack on Israel during its holiest day),[7] Israel realized that it hadn't taken the warning signs seriously enough. Collectively, the people in the government had missed signals that could have allowed them to prepare better for what eventually materialized. As a result, something akin to a "Tenth Man Rule" supposedly came about. The idea as explained in the movie is that if nine leaders in a row agree on a course of action, the tenth, by default, must disagree. This leader must take a "devil's advocate" position, just to challenge incumbent thinking. By taking up a contrarian point of view, the tenth man is able to immunize the group against groupthink and open up everyone's eyes to the broader possibilities.[8,9,10] If everyone else dismisses a possible idea because it's too outlandish, the tenth man will speak up for this contrarian point of view, forcing the group to consider the "what if" scenarios.

If you were always asking, "What are we missing?" you might hear the new employee's ideas with a different set of ears. Sure, they're inexperienced, and they're talking endlessly about some new technology, but maybe they're on to something?

With a tenth man attitude, you'll be more likely to listen in as the marketplace pushes new ideas; the next time someone says that a wave is coming, you may be able to believe them, just for a moment. With a tenth man attitude, you won't fall prey to consensus in investing in career choices. Almost assuredly, by playing devil's advocate, if there is any value to be found in the contrarian's point of view on any topic, you'll have at least considered it.

Always be willing to ask yourself and your team:

WHAT ARE WE MISSING? Maybe the next product, geography, or marketing campaign *seems* obvious, but for a second, take the opposing position and push back.

WHAT IF WE'RE WRONG? When your whole team agrees with something, push back. Pit yourself against groupthink for a moment to explore the alternative. **WHAT IF THEY'RE RIGHT?** Don't be quick to laugh today. Be quick to listen and learn. Maybe someone's idea sounds too far-fetched, but those are the ones that always catch people (and countries) by surprise. As the controversial figure Jordan Peterson says, "Assume that the person you are listening to might know something you don't."[11]

2. START OUT "CREEPY"—IT'S A PREREQUISITE

Innovation typically sneaks up on us. We all live in our safe little castles. We're fortified with traditional thinking, with an echo chamber that continually reinforces what we hope is true, that we've got it all figured out. Our castles of traditionalism are set on hilltops, built out of rock, with guards in the towers. We look out and casually shoot down any new idea that threatens our psychological safety net. But disruption will fly overhead in a jet, or climb up the back end, scaling the impossible cliff, or crawl up from underground and then pop up in the town square. You can't keep it out.

Disruption will always find a way, because it lurks in the darkness. It creeps up in the mist to ambush the status quo with a surprising knife in the back.

I remember when Facebook introduced the newsfeed. Until then, you could "Facebook-stalk" people, but you did it by clicking on their profile and then scanning their wall of information. But when the newsfeed came out, it amalgamated everything every single one of your friends did, all in one place. Nothing was hidden. In one glance, I knew when friends broke up, got together, or changed their views on religion. I knew what everyone said, did, liked, clicked on, or joined, all at the same time. It brought social media stalking to a whole new level.

That level of transparency was creepy, wild, and new. Now it's the standard way we consume content on any platform, even in news or at work. Rewind 20 years ago, and one of the main "problems" with Amazon was that no one thought people would feel comfortable allowing a website to store their credit card information. Tracking friends and family with Find My iPhone, disappearing photos on Snapchat, coworking with people from different companies, meeting online in your own home for work, taking public transportation, buying centralized food from a grocery store instead of a farm—it was all weird, at first.

Be on the lookout for those creepy trends, so you can capitalize on them. Do that by:

- **PAYING ATTENTION TO WHAT MAKES PEOPLE UNCOMFORTABLE.** Listen to the people around you or online. What makes people the most uncomfortable today will become tomorrow's disruption. One of my video editors once said that "TikTok was cringy, and I would never be on it," but now, she posts on TikTok almost every day.
- **JUMPING ON FAST TRENDS.** Develop your innovation muscle by experimenting and trying the newest products and technologies. From Product Hunt, to Reddit, to Twitter, you can find people that are making big leaps in various industries.

3. RECONSIDER WHAT'S "OBVIOUSLY" WRONG

The leaders of the legendary Andreessen Horowitz venture capital firm—who have invested in such wins as Skype, Coinbase, Roblox, and Slack—have a simple trick they use to find genius ideas. After a day of pitches, they stop and ask, "OK, what was the obviously bad idea that was *actually* a good idea?"

Genghis Khan, one of the most feared and ruthless conquerors in history, offers a masterclass in bad ideas that were actually good ideas. Khan's armies were known for their unbelievable skill and prowess when it came to both riding horses and shooting arrows. He made it mandatory for all male children to have exceptional archery and horsemanship skills. One of the most unorthodox and difficult moves was being able to shoot targets while riding backward. At first glance, this looks like a suicide job: You can't even see where you're going! However, this tactic was particularly effective, as it would give the perception that the Mongols would be fleeing away; yet they would still be shooting down their enemies. His obviously bad ideas helped him conquer more land than any other leader did in world history.

It's easy to dismiss things that are clearly unconventional, and society's made a game out of looking smart by being cynical. But often what we're so quick to dismiss becomes central to our lives. At first it was clearly a bad idea. Later we're wondering how we missed it.

When you're willing to step into the obviously wrong mindset, no matter how laughable it immediately seems, you may find a gold mine of hidden insights. I'm not sure there's a true "hack" to innovation, but if there were, it would be to constantly ask yourself, "What's the obviously bad idea that's a hidden good idea?"

IT ONLY TAKES ONE HIT

The inherent issue with the Contrarian Matrix is that you must always start out as a contrarian. You must first risk going against the consensus. Ominously, you may still be incorrect, in which case the joke was always on you. Clearly, the consensus isn't always wrong, right?

Just because an idea is trumpeted by the masses doesn't mean it's wrong. But the important thing to remember is that you can only drive value when you're a contrarian and you're right. If you're a betting person, you should bet *against* the crowd as much as possible, without totally alienating yourself.

Jeff Bezos is famous for disrupting the way Americans shop for everything. What he's less famous for are his flops. Here's a snapshot of his absolute failures:

- Crucible (a $60 million video game platform flop)
- LivingSocial (after Amazon invested $175 million and faced multiple lawsuits, it quite literally gave the company to Groupon)
- Pets.com ($50 million failed investment)
- Kozmo.com ($60 million failed investment)
- Amazon Destinations, Amazon Auctions, zShops, Amazon Local register, Amazon Test Drive, Amazon WebPay, . . .

To summarize, as Bezos told the folks at the Business Insider Ignition conference: "I've made billions of dollars of failures at Amazon.com." Bezos has fallen on his face—hard. But countering, he's also said, "A single big winning bet can more than cover the cost of many losers."[12] In other words, one grand slam outweighs dozens of strikeouts.

Being a contrarian is a prerequisite to disruption. You must be willing to be the joke once, twice, or even 10 times before you ever get a hit. And then if you want to keep getting hits, you must keep striking out. Not everyone has the stomach for such a failure rate. But, as Bezos pointed out, the alternative is that we can all get caught off guard one day, surprised by a disruption in our lives, careers, or business, and *then* be forced into a one-shot Hail Mary to save everything.

Maybe you're a quantitative analyst and you're sensing that the world will soon shift to a higher dependence on *qualitative* analysis. What could you do to be on the front lines of that change, instead of being swept away by it? You could experiment with a marriage of quantitative and qualitative analysis, or perhaps you could discover a way to pool qualitative opinions and turn them into data. Your first idea may not work, but if you disrupt your own role before the market does, you'll stand to gain, and you won't be forced to learn a new bag of tricks all at once. In fact, you might just be the one creating that bag of new tricks.

TRY TO GET YOURSELF FIRED

Here's a contrarian habit I created when I worked at Deloitte: I would walk into work every single day and ask this question:

What can I do to get myself fired today?

I didn't do anything violent or illegal, but I wanted to make a dangerous move in a positive direction that would create massive action. I wanted to build my innovation muscle so I had enough swings to get a hit. Here's what I found—I never got fired. You won't either.

Try to get yourself fired, find out that it won't happen, and you'll be set up for the next big thing. Because, here's the deal: hits are your *job*. In the end, it's all of our jobs to create a smash hit.

WHAT WILL PEOPLE SAY?

As a South Asian and second-generation immigrant, I heard the following saying countless times growing up (if you're a second-generation immigrant in North America, you've heard it too):

What will people say?

I've never seen four words crush an entire generation of young people more than those have.

I have seen that questions destroy the potential careers of athletes, creatives, and artists, block potential marriages, and keep people in relationships they wanted to leave. The immigrant community often celebrates the slow and steady. So, they encourage each other to choose law over acting, break up with someone for being in a different social status, or choose medicine as a career over athletics.

Regardless of your heritage, you've probably heard that saying as well, or at least felt its impact in your own life. What others will think of us holds us back. As an added punch, this question often arises just before a soon-to-be Bold One is about to take their first step into disruption, out of the status quo; they don't have any clout, conviction, credibility, or confidence yet, so their defenses are down.

I have a few ideas on how to fortify yourself against this dream-killing question:

- **PRACTICE ACCEPTING TROLLS AND THEIR COMMENTS.**
  People will laugh at you, but remember, everyone's

a comedian, until it's time to be funny. Lighten up. Laugh at your own failures too. Embrace the trolls, and turn their negativity into something funny. Compliment them even; because remember, you'll get the last laugh.

• **KEEP GOING.** Others will doubt you. The best way to prove the doubters wrong is to increase your momentum. The very moment someone doubts you, or you fail, or you hear the dreaded "What will people say?" question, take immediate and decisive action. Don't let their skepticism seep into your conscious.

Back in Edmonton, my Canadian school had what most schools have: a valedictorian, a salutatorian, and a class president. I wasn't any of those, but I *was* selected to be one of the three class historians. To me, it was prestigious work.

Into my final year, I put my heart and soul into my historian role. With my three colleagues, Rahul, Jameel, and Michael, we created an elaborate video performance for graduation. The work consumed me. My mother kept asking, "Why are you spending so much time working on that computer?"

I tried to explain to her how important this project was to me, my cohistorians, and the school, but she just didn't get it. Until graduation.

When the big day came, the Jubilee Theater, which seats about 2,400 people, was packed with students, family members, and loved ones. It was the perfect setting for parents (particularly immigrant parents) to show off how intelligent their children are. The valedictorian gave her speech, the class president probably read a quote, and the principal tried to inspire. But you know what the talk of the day was?

Our historian video performance.

My team murdered it.

I couldn't have been prouder with our product, or the response. Over 2,000 people were teary-eyed, everyone laughed, and the compliments rolled in all night.

Oh, and my parents finally understood. They were ecstatic. The praise and the attention from the evening became a defining moment for my adult life. My team's success was so infectious and penetrating, that today I essentially do the same thing with my speeches—offer life-size media-rich presentations that I (and my family) can be immensely proud of.

If you want to inspire, it doesn't hurt to show some wins. You'll be a joke at first. In fact, if you aren't, you might not be thinking big enough. You'll need some boldness to step into the unknown. But somewhere along the way, you'll need to convince others. And you do that by showing them. Fight against the "What will people say?" mentality, and move forward with your conviction.

JAMSETJI'S LAST LAUGH

Jamsetji Tata died in 1904. When he did, he left behind the beginning of an empire. Later, in 1930, Mahatma Gandhi would help inspire the peaceful end of British occupation. Famously, the last British occupying troops left from India's Gateway to India, a monument right across the plaza from Jamsetji's Taj Mahal Hotel—the same one he built out of spite. Now, every day, guests of the world-famous Taj Mahal Palace (the hotel changed its name in 2003) can stare at the monument dedicated to the end of imperialism and the beginning of a self-ruled, modern nation.

But the irony gets better. Tata's great-grandson, Ratan Tata, who rose through the ranks of the Tata companies, eventually became chairman of his family's empire in 1991. Under his leadership, Tata purchased three *British* companies: Tetley, Jaguar Land Rover, and Anglo-Dutch Corus Group.

The man who used innovation to upend imperialism begat a descendant who, through a global free market, placed *British* enterprises under *Indian* ownership. Who got the last laugh? Remember:

Disruption is a joke. Until the joke's on them.

SECRETS OF THE BOLD ONES

RECOGNIZE THAT DISRUPTION OFTEN STARTS AS A JOKE. When the masses first hear of a good idea in disguise, they often respond with laughter. Only Bold Ones who are willing to be laughed at—at least initially—can disrupt and get the last laugh.

BE A CONTRARIAN. Only contrarians win big. There is very little reward for going with the consensus, even if you're right. Only by going against the grain and being correct can you win big.

BE THE "TENTH MAN." The tenth man is the person who's always willing to be the devil's advocate. Your company's, your team's, and even your own immune system may kick in and reject a good idea. Be willing to pretend, at least for a moment, that a crazy, contrarian idea has merit. Only then will you be able to determine whether it does.

UNDERSTAND THAT CREEPY IS A PREREQUISITE TO INNOVATION. Innovation always starts out a bit weird. Think of Airbnb—who on earth would want strangers in their home? Too often we reject ideas out of hand because they feel strange. But almost all innovation starts that way.

RECONSIDER WHAT'S "OBVIOUSLY" WRONG. Always be willing to take a second look at what was dismissed as a clearly bad idea. In fact, most disruptions were considered horrible ideas at one time.

REMEMBER THAT IT ONLY TAKES ONE HIT. As a contrarian, you can afford to be wrong nine times out of ten. One big, contrarian win will outweigh all other instances of failure.

CHAPTER 6

INNOVATION'S DIRTY LITTLE SECRET

Michele Romanow leaned forward in her chair and listened intently to the deal. At this point, she'd heard about 250 of these pitches over the last few weeks.

The founders in front of her—a father-and-son duo—had a great idea, a great business model, and great execution. They'd already sold about $1 million of their wooden iPhone cases. The metrics were excellent: $10 to make, $10 to advertise, $50 to sell. A proven, safe investment. At the end of their seven-minute pitch, they made their ask.

They wanted $100,000 in cash in exchange for giving the investors a 20 percent stake in their company.

Romanow sat back. *That's a bad deal for everyone*, she thought.

A company in a small niche like iPhone cases wasn't shooting for a high-dollar exit—the kind that investors are hungry for. Instead, this family outfit was likely to sit back and enjoy healthy profit margins and a steady stream of income and keep their small corner of the market on lock. But exiting for anything in the "illions" wasn't in their future (nor necessarily what they wanted). Plus, no small business owner wanted to give up nearly a quarter of their enterprise—they'd eventually grow resentful and regretful of their investors.

The father-and-son pitch wasn't a great deal, but it also wasn't unique. It was pretty similar to the hundreds that Romanow had already heard during the last two to three weeks of filming: An established business needed cash to scale, and the investors would take advantage, offering liquidity for large equity stakes. But this time, even the other investors wouldn't be interested in such a small deal.

So Romanow sat up and offered a bold, new type of arrangement.

She'd give the family the $100,000, but she wouldn't take *any* equity. Instead, the money would be a loan, with modest interest. The father and son were elated and quickly agreed. The only caveat? Romanow wanted to take a peek at their social media engagement.

If you didn't know any better, it may be easy to discount her move as naïve—after all, she was the youngest investor ever on *Dragons' Den*, the Canadian version of America's *Shark Tank*. Other "dragons" invited on the show would include mostly older men, such as Lane Merrifield, cofounder of the $600 million company Club Penguin (acquired by Disney), and Kevin "Mr. Wonderful" O'Leary.

Romanow knew what it was like to be a young, hungry entrepreneur who couldn't get investment dollars. At 21, she'd tried to disrupt the most unlikely of businesses—caviar. It blew up in her face. But she then went to Sears as their director of strategy, and eventually started an e-commerce platform called "Buytopia." Later she also started SnapSaves, which she sold to Groupon for twice its valuation.

She'd had a hard time getting cash from investors to bankroll social media ads for Buytopia, even though she had a proven conversion plan. So she used the last dollar in her personal bank account to buy the ads.

When she joined *Dragons' Den* four years later in 2015, she heard from various other entrepreneurs that they were in the same boat—they had a proven business, with a tried-and-true conversion strategy, but they still couldn't get the money they needed for their social media campaigns. So they'd turn to expensive money from investors—like the dragons—for the needed cash to scale.

The show films all the pitches in about a two- to three-week period, so Romanow had seen this go down over 200-plus times already. When she heard the father-and-son pitch, she had a lightbulb moment—*why does the most expensive cash a founder will likely ever access go straight to what should be the most scalable, replicable part of a business?* For investors, if the ad campaign was good, this was about as close to a guarantee as they could get— meaning it *should* be the cheapest and easiest loan for a founder.

No one likely realized it then, but Romanow had just offered the first $100,000 of a new billion-dollar investment industry, one based not on the haggling of sharky investors, but on hard data, social media campaigns, and low interest rates.

She took a lose-lose deal and turned it into a win-win by discovering something no one else could see.

About two years after that first deal, Romanow cofounded Clearco, on the same premise, to fund scalable marketing campaigns for established companies. The owner walks away with all their equity intact and still in control, while Clearco walks away with a predictable ROI.

To date, Clearco has funded 7,000 companies with a total of $3 billion.

By listening to 250 or so pitches, Romanow had discovered a small, simple secret, one that was out there for the taking, but that no one truly grasped: New businesses wanted money for predictable ads. Investors want predictable ROI. It should have been a match made in heaven. Instead, it became a match made in the *Dragons' Den.*

DISRUPTION = ~~INVENT~~ DISCOVER

Isaac Newton didn't invent gravity; he *discovered* it. It had been there all along, embedded in the DNA of physics. When you find a secret, just like Newton, you unlock something that changes the world.

That's what a secret is: a truth waiting in plain sight, buried by psychological hindrances and status quo traditionalism. Once someone points it out, the palm hits the face (or the apple hits the head). *Why couldn't we all see that?* When you find that secret, it unleashes power in the marketplace (and dollars in the bank account).

I was recently playing around with TikTok's ad platform when I discovered a small secret to targeting. Today most social platforms won't allow you to target your ads by ethnicity. I get why, but as a South Asian Canadian, many of my truest fans are fellow South Asians. They write notes like, "Love seeing another brown guy doing his thing." I wanted to reach this group in a scalable method to invite them to one of my upcoming shows. It dawned on me: I could target by hashtags like #browntiktok, #Bollywood, or #punjabi. (Almost) anyone following those will be South Asian.

I tested my idea with $18 in ads. I got over 50 conversions, one of the best ROIs I'd ever seen using paid social media marketing.

Some secrets, like the TikTok hashtag, are small, leading to individual value. Others, like Romanow's, are game changing and create entire industries

In this chapter, we're going to take a look at the role secrets play in disruption. Here's what we'll unpack:

- **THE ROI ON SECRETS.** Research shows that ROI is highest for companies on the most transformative initiatives. Yet, companies invest most of their money on incremental improvements. Instead, they should invest in "secrets," discovering new ideas that can transform companies and industries.
- **THERE ARE THREE LAYERS OF SECRETS.** Obvious secrets, hard-to-find secrets, and the deepest dark secrets. As you descend into another layer, you discover more and more value. The more difficult and less obvious a secret is, the more value it holds
- **THE DIRTY TRUTH.** Ivory towers don't discover secrets; practitioners do. To find a secret, you've got to get dirty. Be on the front lines, listen intently, get "in the weeds" on a subject, topic, or line of work.

By the end, you'll have some tools to discover secrets at each layer, which will allow you to add to your own innovation.

THE ROI ON SECRETS

Some of my colleagues at Monitor Deloitte[1] did a large-scale study on innovation. They researched the market, and they found that institutions had three options when considering where to invest their resources:

1. Optimize their core basket of offerings.
2. Invest in new solutions that were different from the current offering, but not truly disruptive.
3. Invest in transformational initiatives that would typically require a high level of research and development (or at least much thought, buy-in, and potential risk).

From there, they wanted to find out, "In what category do companies spend their resources? And from what category do they drive the most return on investment?"

Similar to the Contrarian Matrix in the previous chapter, as you may guess, the study showed that well over two-thirds of all new value comes from transformational initiatives. If you were an investor, it would make sense to put your money there. But in practice, companies invest in the exact *opposite* manner, giving only 10 percent of all resources to this category, opting instead to play it safe and invest in nondisruptive offerings.

Borrowing from their study, and from the work of Peter Thiel, I've created the Iceberg of Secrecy, shown in Figure 6.1. Essentially, secrets can indeed be categorized into three groups, with each one representing a different increase in value when discovered:

1. **OBVIOUS SECRETS.** These secrets are hidden in plain sight and give you a jump-start on disruption.
2. **HARD-TO-FIND SECRETS.** These are the second-layer secrets; finding these is harder, and requires you to take a deeper look into human psychology and habits.
3. **DEEPEST AND DARKEST SECRETS.** These are the real game changers, potentially driving millions of dollars' worth of innovation. To find these, you'll need to think, watch, think again, and watch again.

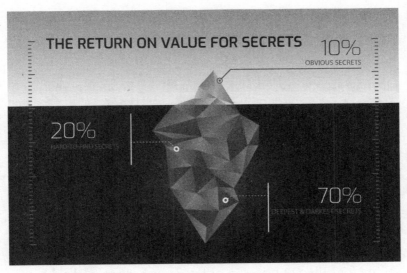

FIGURE 6.1 The return on value for the three layers of secrets. Overall, the total value you can derive from innovation is composed of the three types of secrets.

If you live a bold, dangerous life full of disruption, by the end, finding obvious secrets will have unlocked about 10 percent of that value. Hard-to-find secrets will compose about

20 percent. Finally, a few deep and dark secrets will make up the vast majority—up to 70 percent—of all the value you ever derive from innovation.

Your ability to disrupt rests disproportionately on uncovering deep, dark secrets, and of course, these are the hardest to mine.

There isn't an exact formula for how to allocate your time, energy, and resources; occasionally, you should take baby steps to gain some quick, easy wins. However, it's also important to keep the whole "iceberg" in mind—and remember that if you want to really change the game in your life, your company, or your industry, you'll need to get deep.

LAYER 1: OBVIOUS SECRETS

Obvious secrets are loopholes—small little anomalies that, once exploited, offer immediate and real value. While these typically make up only 10 percent of the long-term value of innovation, don't ignore them. They can be massively beneficial, particularly in the short run.

Sam Bankman-Fried (SBF) is the youngest billionaire in the world. He got there by exploiting something so obvious, it's difficult to even call it hidden. He looked at the crypto exchanges in various countries and discovered that the same crypto was selling for different prices in different exchanges. So he'd buy in the United States and sell in Japan, or buy in Russia and sell in Germany, and so on. Soon he automated this process with rules and protocols, so his wealth just kept growing like the predictable swing of a pendulum. Today SBF is a multibillionaire, the CEO of FTX, and one of the most innovative leaders in the Web3 space.

An obvious secret can be as small as my TikTok discovery. There are little automations hidden in Excel files, slight adjustments to your customer experience, or fine-tuning in your marketing process that can unlock benefit for relatively little effort. Dan Martell, founder and CEO of SaaS Academy, says that he's seen just *one word* in a marketing campaign dramatically change the ROI.

Here's what I love about obvious secrets: They're everywhere, and they're available to everyone.

An obvious secret can kick-start your innovation brain. They're like juicy, quick wins, powerful enough to entice you further down the rabbit hole of innovation, but temporary enough to leave you wanting more.

Over time, these little tweaks create massive value either by showcasing a broader pattern, or by simply seducing you even further down the rabbit hole.

Here are a few places to start your journey down the rabbit hole of innovation:

ASK BOLDER QUESTIONS

If you want *answers*, ask Alexa. If you want to find *secrets*, start by asking bolder questions. Start with the surface-level questions, the ones that feel almost too obvious to even ask. While these may vary by industry, here's some good ones:

- "Do we really need to use this so-called best practice?"
- "Why do we use this process, strategy, or method?
- "Can I streamline or automate some part of this process?"

CONSIDER THE DETAILS

Lowes Foods is an American grocery store chain. At one of their newest stores in Huntersville, North Carolina, Disneyland-esque decorations greet you at every station, while the employees wear highly themed uniforms depending on their department. On weekends, the store has live music. In the center, there's a bar, with craft brews that rotate. Parents can pop a beer, listen to great music, and grocery-shop, all with a kid in the shopping cart. In the cake department, whimsical colors, decorations, and enticing items abound. In the corner, there's a book of possible cake creations, with a single step just beneath it, so children can step up and turn the pages themselves.

Each of these details creates a profound customer experience, and each invites customers to stay longer, shop more, and return frequently. The details of the experience bring it to life.

In your own role, in your own life, think of the small, hidden ways you can create additional value for your customers, your audience, or your company. For example:

- Is there a small amount of automation you can add that will take your work from good to great?
- Perhaps you're a sales rep; can you make a piece of content that handles clients' top-10 objections even *before* they ask them?
- Does your boss have a consistent weak spot that you can recognize that you can fill politely, to complement their work?

In these little ways, you can start to drive real value, build your own innovation muscle, and start to learn how to mine deeper secrets.

LAYER 2: HARD-TO-FIND SECRETS

The next layer of secrets is more difficult to discover. While you'll find obvious secrets snooping around the edges of your own role, if you want to find the next-level secrets, you'll have to go outside your entire company to dig deeper into the customer psyche. You'll need to ask:

- "How are others observing what's going on?"
- "How do they see the value I'm providing?"
- "How easy/difficult is their experience?"
- "What are ways I can improve that experience?"
- "What is the end user *really* looking for?"

A case in point: In the late 1960s, coffee wasn't just a commodity; it was an afterthought. The proverbial intern or assistant was responsible for keeping the pot boiling at the office, and you could pop into a 7-Eleven for a pick-me-up for under a buck.

Howard Schultz was watching Americans drink lots of coffee, but none of it was very high in quality. He visited Italy to learn from world-renowned coffee roasters. He then considered how to increase the shelf life of coffee beans across the United States. Many of these were small, perhaps even obvious, adjustments. But then a game changer occurred in how he looked at the end-user experience. By watching customers and their consumption habits during his first trip to Milan, he was "captivated by the sense of community" at the espresso bars between the staff and its customers.

Plus, while customers in America were paying pennies for coffee, no food item there was as customized as one's coffee: Emily likes it with no sugar and a bit of cream, Brandon wants his with three sugars and lots of cream, and Nick takes his with two Splendas, no cream. People who order filet mignon at high-end restaurants aren't even that choosy.

So, Schultz repositioned Starbucks's latte, and the coffee experience in general, as a luxury purchase. A special drink, and indeed an experience, worth the spend. Utilizing these secrets, Schultz built an empire of 31,000 stores across 80 different countries.

In your own industry, if you want to upgrade from just making minor tweaks in your own role to capitalizing on how others behave, you'll need to dig a little deeper and discover something more profound.

Here are a few ways to unlock those hard-to-find secrets:

FOLLOW PEOPLE AROUND

Henry Ford famously said, "If I had asked people what they wanted, they would have said faster horses." Users have no clue what they want. If you ask them, they'll offer a theory. At best, that theory will be obvious; and at worst, they'll tell you to train faster horses.

Instead, stalk customers. In a noncreepy way, of course. I mean to truly observe human behavior. Only then will you discover how people think and how they operate.

- What are they doing on the subway to work?
- Could you make their commute more efficient?
- Is there a way to eliminate friction in their internet searches?
- What is it about their favorite meeting spot that makes it so desirable?
- How do people stand in line at their favorite lunch spot?
- At what time are there lulls on the highway?

I want you to follow people around in the wild. Literally. Systematically document in depth the details of your customers or audience. From speech to habits to facial expressions, the deepest secrets are in the most mundane actions.

As a final tip: Record everything. Every year, we're blessed with seemingly better video quality. In the most ethical way possible, record your subjects, events, or settings, and let the video run.

PAY ATTENTION TO WEIRD HABITS

In the last chapter, we talked about not dismissing the odd, strange, or even "creepy" ideas, as they may just be weird enough to work. But now turn your attention to human *behavior*. Are customers or colleagues in your field consistently behaving in an odd way?

- Does virtually every customer make the same mistake when interacting with your software?
- Have you noticed that people always walk in a certain fashion when they come into work?
- In the broader marketplace, can you see a psychological trend stemming from how people search for a topic?

At first, just pay attention. Sometimes the answers don't have an immediate payoff, but it's good practice to build your secret-hunting skills. And people's odd habits often stem from a deeper psychological need.

REPOSITION A PRODUCT OR SERVICE

You can find a ton of value by taking a necessity and making it exciting and desirable. The repositioning of coffee, from a commodity to a luxury product, was key for Starbucks. After observing customer behaviors, Schultz was able to understand that the product everyone saw as cheap was actually an in-demand item that they habitually craved and to a high level of specificity. So, he flipped the script, turning commodity coffee into luxury lattes.

Look outside your daily routine to consider how your value is perceived by the marketplace. With new lenses on, can you reposition your product or service, and capitalize on that value?

Say you're an accountant—what some see as a commodity, but truthfully, you're a necessity. As you crunch numbers all day, you may be able to find small ways to speed up your process, automate your findings, or unlock processes that compound over time. Obvious secrets.

But then, what if you took a step backward and considered how valuable the insights you're driving really are? Could you reposition your role from the service they must pay for to the partnership that increases revenue? With unique access to raw data, you can exactly where resources are being underutilized, or where money could be invested differently to increase revenue streams. You know about hidden inefficiencies, redundancies, and untapped resources. If you can change the perception of your value, you could reposition yourself from bookkeeper to advisor—and likely triple or quadruple your fee.

As a tip: Intellectual laziness or marketing hype simply won't cut it here. Only reposition yourself for the value that already exists.

––––––––––

Obvious secrets provide the jump-starts to innovation, and usually, you find them by considering your daily work. However, take it up a notch, and start observing your customers' behaviors and needs. That's usually where you'll find the more valuable secrets. If you can make changes (or reposition yourself) to better execute on a needed or wanted service or product, you can find increased value.

LAYER 3: DEEPEST, DARKEST SECRETS

You only find deep, dark secrets when you walk so far into the jungle, you've wandered outside your own industry. Now, you're considering how trends are building across industries and patterns are emerging. When you seek out the commonalities underlying seemingly unrelated developments, you may just stumble upon something so universal, so central to the terrestrial experience, that you create a new world.

It takes a true scholar, journalist, or scientist to understand these broad trends. But you don't need letters after your name to be a scientist, at least not when it comes to innovation. You just need to observe closely:

- What's the connecting point between new government policies and developments in music?
- Is there an underlying ingredient between pop culture and economics?
- How does the emergence of social media relate to an increase in solopreneurs?

Most credit Cai Lun as a key ingredient in the world's development of modern paper. Instead of silk, he suggested to the Chinese emperor that tree bark and other ingredients could be combined to create an inexpensive, replicable, and writable surface. Where did he get his idea? Supposedly from observing wasps and how they make their homes.

Here you have a Chinese eunuch serving the palace by producing instruments and weapons, and he stumbles upon one of the greatest innovations in history, one that didn't just change an industry, but humanity. A deep, dark secret of mass communication, discovered by watching insects.

Tough questions take a real journalist willing to follow the story, even if it isn't quite clear where it's going. Dr. Isaac Asimov, a biochemist and award-winning science fiction writer, once said this:

> **The most exciting phrase to hear in science,**
> **the one that heralds new discoveries,**
> **is not "Eureka!" but "That's funny . . . ."**

Often you're not quite sure what you're looking for. You're opening the hatches to various compartments and just exploring disparate fringes. You're asking open-ended questions, not quite sure where they'll lead, if anywhere at all.

If you know what you're looking for, then you'll find it. But be willing to dig so deep that instead of understanding what you see, your first reaction is, "That's funny . . . ."

Creating a "That's funny" experience is difficult, but I have two tactics that can help:

- **EXPLORE WITHOUT EXPECTATION.** You know what I love about kids? They do things "just because." Adults have traded playtime for work time, and it keeps us from discovery. Sometimes we just need to play, to click, to research, read, visit, and explore, all without an agenda. Set aside an hour or two every week to research a new topic, simply because you're interested in it. Make exploration the *goal*, not the means to an end.

- **CONNECT THE DOTS.** Here's an experiment for you: Look at changes happening in two disparate industries—say, social media and banking—and try to see if you can find one singular rule about human behavior that is causing both changes. If you can relate the disruptive happenings from two different worlds and boil them down to a singular component, perhaps you can then apply that component to *another* industry to predict the next disruption.

THE DIRTY TRUTH

There is one more thing I didn't mention about Clearco.

Interestingly, because of Romanow's innovative intervention into banking, she solved one of the industry's leading problems: She eliminated gender bias.

At Clearco a human is essentially uninvolved with the decision to fund or not fund a business. Instead, just as Romanow requested from that first deal, Clearco wants a peek at your social media, and now, it's all automated. If your social media campaigns have ROI, Clearco gives you funding.

Since no humans are involved, a positive side effect of this automation is that women-owned companies receive more investment money than the industry standard, because their process eliminates human bias and potential sexism from the process. By 2022, Clearco bragged that it funded at least 10 times more women than the average VC fund did.

People had discussed the issue of sexism in funding for decades.

They talked about it, Romanow solved it.

She did it by getting her fingers dirty.

When Romanow discovered the secret to unlocking Clearco's billion-dollar investment strategy, she was in the trenches, day after day, listening to pitch after pitch in the *Dragons' Den,* a name that showcases exactly how deep and dark you really must go to unearth the diamonds in the mine. In the den, you may find a lot of useless coal, maybe even some danger. But eventually you'll discover a gem.

So get *dirty*.

SECRETS OF THE BOLD ONES

INVEST IN DISCOVERY. Companies spend most of their time on incremental adjustments and changes. However, the greatest value lies in discovering secrets, not in making small changes to preexisting products and services. The deeper you dig, the greater the value.

JUMP-START YOUR INNOVATION BRAIN BY FINDING OBVIOUS SECRETS. Look for tiny automations or small changes you can make to your process that can unlock value in your day-to-day work.

OBSERVE HUMAN BEHAVIOR FOR HARD-TO-FIND SECRETS. Follow humans around to understand why they do what they do. Remember, don't ask them to tell you; they don't understand themselves. Instead, observe, follow, and ponder. In particular, pay attention to humanity's oddest habits.

CONSIDER CHANGES OUTSIDE YOUR INDUSTRY TO DISCOVER DEEPEST, DARKEST SECRETS. The most radical discoveries are made when you go outside your own industry and consider broader trends in human behavior, or how an idea can be borrowed from one field and placed into a new context.

GET DIRTY. To find valuable secrets, you have to be willing to get your fingers dirty, in the clay. Tinker with the details; ask open-ended questions. The greatest discoveries are made without an agenda.

CHAPTER 7

ONE TRUE FAN

In 1995, Mary Meeker released "The Internet Report," a 200-page document outlining trends on the internet. Perhaps for the first time on a broad scale, this report brought financial data on internet-based companies to the public. This was information that typically only investors could see or comprehend. Her simple, comprehensive, and digestible format thrust Meeker center stage, recognized not only by those in the tech industry, but by the average individual as well.

Working as an analyst at Morgan Stanley, Meeker saw the internet's potential and was convinced of its financial potency. Her report, which named what she believed would be future winners in the coming internet era, became the stock-picking guide for many. Offering data, graphs, and charts and presented in an understandable format, the report became a lasting, annual legacy that thousands looked forward to every year.

Then came the internet crash of 2000.

Fortune magazine put Meeker on its cover in 2001 along with the question, "Can we ever trust Wall Street again?"

Meeker didn't back down. She pressed on with her report, believing in the inevitable rise of the internet. Despite the potential backlash, she remained steadfast. Every year, she continued to go through her hundreds-plus–page document, evangelizing the internet, highlighting cultural shifts and their impact.

She survived, thrived, and is still thriving. Today she's known as "Queen of the Internet," a title *Barron's* magazine bestowed upon her in 1998. Just like the royal Elizabeth II, when the Queen of the Internet spoke, people paid attention. Meeker eventually left Morgan Stanley and started her own venture capitalist firm, Bond Capital. Now she's calling the shots as the ruler of her own land. In 2012, *Time* named her one of the 10 most influential women in technology.

Meeker focused on a fringe idea (the internet), built her own IP, kept chipping away at it, and eventually built a lasting legacy from her unique interests.

In Chapter 4, we discussed the paradox of piracy—*why* focusing on a few is the path to massive disruption. Consider this Part II of that discussion. Here we're going to get a little more tactical. We're going to zoom in from the paradigm shift, and take you to the actionable.

1,000 TRUE FANS? TRY JUST ONE

The romantic narrative about disruption is "the moment"—the moment the iPhone launched, the moment Elon Musk landed his shuttle vertically, the moment Mary Meeker hit "publish" on her first Internet Trends Report. Opportunistic moments of popularity do come (we'll talk about them in the next chapter), but those windows of time are created from action, repetition, and consistency.

Disruptors are relentlessly determined people who continually execute. They remain loyal to their supporters, and when bumps come, they don't stop.

When we talked about creating a cult in Chapter 4, you may have wondered, "How many followers do I need?" My suggestion is that the number is very, very small. In fact, it's close to zero.

But before I get to *my* number, let's start with Kevin Kelly's number: 1,000.

In 2008, Kelly wrote a now-famous essay entitled "1,000 True Fans."[1] In it, he suggested that to find success doing what you love, you don't need a massive following. You just need 1,000 dedicated individuals.

He actually put the math behind it: If 1,000 people pay you $100 a year, then you'd make $100,000 annually. His concept was fresh, his wording was catchy, and the idea spread like fire among his followers.

Remember, when Kelly wrote that, it was, as noted, 2008. He wasn't truly identifying an exact number; he was identifying a trend occurring in the technosphere: Technology exponentially increases the value of our connections, continually eliminating gatekeepers that would keep leaders from their fans. Every technology connects us more—from the radio, to television, to the computer, to the internet, to the smartphone. With each innovation, another barrier between one human and another falls, and the value of each connection intensifies.

In 2008, technology had advanced to a degree that you only needed 1,000 people to make noise in the market, get noticed, and get paid. Twelve years later, in 2020, Li Jin, famous for coining the phrase "passion economy," went even further in her own essay, called "100 True Fans."[2] Her argument? Kelly was right. But that was over a decade before she wrote *her* essay. Jin posited that by 2020, more and more people—both fans and creators—had jumped on the passion economy bandwagon. She noted that people were paying more to learn skills from peers (like how to master chess), were buying unique creations more frequently (like pottery or art), and were shelling out hundreds to hang with their idols (like playing video games with well-known champions). Instead of needing 1,000 true fans willing to pay 100 bucks each, Jin suggested you only needed 100 true fans willing to shell out a grand.

But we're not in 2020 anymore.

Welcome to the age of *1*.

I'm not suggesting that 1 fan will literally pay your bills, but that one fan can make a sizable contribution to your innovation game. We'll unpack what this means in this chapter. But let me be abundantly clear . . .

If you want to disrupt the world, you need 1 insane fan, serving as a mini-cult-following who champions you, your ideas, and your products and services.

Here's how you build this mini-cult, step by step:

STEP 1. DECLARE INDEPENDENCE. First, to build your own party of one, you must build your own personal brand, apart from the company you work at. Continue in your role with all the diligence possible, but people must know *your* name.

STEP 2. CREATE SOMETHING CATCHY. Give your supporters something they can latch onto: a word, a

128

phrase, a sexy angle. Think about what the headline on your project would be, and lead with that, even if it isn't related to the core idea itself.

STEP 3. OVERDELIVER TO THE ONE FAN. Exceed people's expectations, whether that's personally responding to every message or inviting fans to share the stage with you somewhere. Make it costly on you: People remember what costs you something.

Once we investigate those three steps, we'll explore one more idea: Web 3.0. I'm going to break down this phenomenon. People are talking about it, but they're not explaining it. Don't worry—it's actually simple.

STEP 1. DECLARE INDEPENDENCE

So how do we take advantage of this era of one? We've got to be known for something, separate of our careers and our employers. In a phrase, we must *declare independence*.

One of my colleagues at Deloitte, we'll call him "Hitch," is a god in his field. He'd spent over a decade on his craft, and his expertise and intuition surpassed that of any of his peers. When Deloitte reorganized its staff and let him go, Hitch should have easily been able to find a new gig, but it was harder than he thought. The problem?

No one knew him.

He'd been so heads-down in his craft, he'd never bothered to highlight his own work. When he was let go, he had no recognition, and all his greatest ideas had been branded "Deloitte," not "Hitch."

I took his experience as a warning. While giving Deloitte my absolute best efforts, I built my personal brand equity. To me, it's the greatest job security. The corporate world can be fickle, unpredictable, and overly reliant on broad strokes painted by an advisory board. Personal brand equity is also immensely valuable for your employer. When you highlight what you're working on, you're putting signals out into the world that you're proud of your team, your company, and your work. This helps your employer attract top talent, and it's better PR than any company can buy. Since people follow people, one genuine social media post from an excited employee can have ripple effects that far outstretch any mass marketing initiative.

Take CEO James Carbary (mentioned in Chapter 4). He not only *allows* his employees to have their own personal brand; he pays for it, giving all the employees on staff access to Sweet Fish's copywriting team to help them craft social media posts for their own personal pages. Carbary knows that every time his employees boost their personal brand, the company enjoys the by-product of positive association. "They're like mini-billboards," he says.

If Hitch had done what Sweet Fish employees are paid to do, develop his own, independent personal brand, he would have easily been able to find a job after Deloitte. Not only that, but Deloitte itself might have better recognized Hitch's value and never released him in the first place. Likely, because nothing had Hitch's signature on it, the higher-ups didn't really know his worth to the firm. Build your personal brand so you can move when it's time, but with it, you may never need to.

DON'T WORRY ABOUT
WHO "OWNS" THE IP

When you do create something at your traditional workplace, you may wonder, "Who owns the IP?" Technically, your firm may own the IP, depending on the type of work you do and your agreement. But that's not the point. Having your name attached to the IP is the key. In fact, IP that involves *your* brand, name, and energy is probably worthless without you. Remember Simmons's Grantland? After ESPN fired him, they closed the website.

STEP 2. CREATE SOMETHING CATCHY

Ralph Waldo Emerson once said, "Put the argument into a concrete shape, into an image, some hard phrase, round and solid as a ball, which they can see and handle and carry home with them."

In other words, you've got to have an angle that people can latch onto mentally and then "toss" to others. You've got to create something "catchy."

Mary Meeker became the Queen of the Net with a report. Easy to understand and, importantly, easy to share.

It would be far too difficult for one fan to communicate to another, "Hey, you should listen to the wisdom of this investor; she understands a lot about data, the internet, graphs, marketplace trends, and how all that impacts the daily ROI of your investments into technological advancements."

If you tried to say all that, you'd lose someone two seconds in.

Instead, Meeker created something more catchy, something shareable—her report.

When I think of something catchy, I like to think about Barack Obama's 2008 campaign for US president. It was historic for many reasons, not the least of which were his race and ethnicity—he was running to become the first African American president of the most powerful country in the world, one started by mostly white men, many of whom owned black slaves. Plus, he had an odd childhood, being raised in multiple countries, in a mixed-race household, and even living with his grandparents for a time.

His story's inspirational, but to get voters to turn out and supporters to turn up, you don't have time to read them that whole bio. You've got to get the best parts of the story down to something simple.

Created by artist Shepard Fairey, the solution came in a poster with one word on it: HOPE. Fairey's design blended red and blue hues together with a pensive Obama looking upward. That poster caught on like wildfire across the country. It's an easy symbol to point to, and it helps others catch the idea quickly.

Likewise, "Make America Great Again" became the catchy saying Donald Trump used in his own campaign several years later.

Whether you're creating a service, a product, or a political campaign, you've got to consider the shareable angle. Just ask yourself, "What's the thing that people would put in the headlines about this project?" On one consulting project at Deloitte, my team and I were developing new approaches for revenue generation at the government's provincial parks. In itself, that's not the sexiest project. I may have already put you to sleep just bringing it up.

But there *was* a shareable angle of the project: We opted to use drones to create footage. Did we really need the drones? No. But drones were all the rage then, in 2017. Because we used them, people across the firm started talking about what we were doing.

Whether it's a hip visual, a novel technology, or a new method of accomplishing a task, look for the sexy, shareable angle you can insert into your next project. Just like the drone footage, that angle doesn't even need to be related to the core product itself. It just has to be catchy.

DUANE SHOOTS TOYS

Too many people look outside themselves and try to latch onto what's popular. But to get one true fan to really buy into you, you need to dive into *your personal interests.*

I'm friendly with an unbelievable creator who has his own multimedia brand, *Duane Shoots Toys.* Duane has an odd obsession—he's really interested in incredibly detailed figurines and toys. He creates "dioramas"—toy sculptures set up in a particular arrangement in a sort of creative, three-dimensional "scene." For instance, Duane's March 2022 release included a diorama of international soccer superstars Ronaldo and Messi playing a video game together. In another release, his diorama depicted Michael Jordan, Mike Tyson, and Michael Jackson all playing cards together. Each scene is intimate, bursting with color and detail.

It may be odd, but it's what Duane's into. He's amassed millions of subscribers across TikTok, Instagram and YouTube, where he invites others to watch as he creates his dioramas. By tapping into what he loves and sharing it with others, he's managed to create a dedicated following and build his own personal brand.

Here's how you can do the same:

1. **IDENTIFY YOUR MEDIUM.** Whether it's private messages, a weekly email, small-group forums, networking events, stages, social media, or the metaverse, find the medium where your ideas and IP will most likely be embraced.

2. **THROW IN A TWIST.** The best creators are bringing something fundamentally different to the table. Be unique; be different; be contrarian.

3. **MAKE IT EASY.** In *Atomic Habits*, James Clear states that his third law of behavior change is to *make it easy*. Here's the deal: If you want people to catch it, it's got to be easy to receive. Meeker's annual "Internet Trends" report, as it's now called, is a complex document, but you know what's not complex? The name and how the content is delivered. The same with the word "hope." And this isn't just about names. It's about what you create. Try to penetrate the wall of complexity by generating an idea that people can easily catch, and, importantly, easily pass on to the next person.

STEP 3. OVERDELIVER TO THE ONE FAN

So you've completed Step 1: You've declared independence from your employer. And you've completed Step 2: You've created something catchy, something that others can share.

Finally, to get that one superfan who will support you all the way to the end, you've got to do Step 3: Overdeliver to one fan.

Marketing and sales have both become a race to get to "scale." Everywhere businesses are finding new ways to reach as many people with as little effort as possible. We use systems that templatize the emails and then insert someone's name to make it feel like the email was customized. We create virtual classrooms where we record ourselves once and then allow thousands of others to pay for that one video. We blast out tweets so that we can write one note and let millions see it.

I understand the power of some of these tools, but you know what? We're leaving gold on the table when we forget about the importance of one fan.

When you overdeliver value to that one fan, you're treating that fan like they're the only one in the world who matters (because, in that moment, that's true).

So that's the first piece of advice I have: Always, always, acknowledge every fan you can. Then, overdeliver value to them. Here are a few ways to do that:

REPLY TO EVERY COMMENT, EVERY TIME

In the new era, it isn't about having 100 million nameless email addresses. Instead, it's about having an insanely personal touch with one person. For example, I have a total of 12,000+ followers on LinkedIn. And when I've gotten comments, I've managed to reply to every single one.

When a fan takes the time to say, "Hey Shawn! I like the video!" I always (personally!) follow up with something like, "Thanks so much Rodney!" No exceptions.

People love talking to you.

Does it take up time to reply to every single person? Sure.

But it makes people feel special, and that's priceless. (So far, I haven't missed personally replying to one comment!)

SHARE THE STAGE AND YOUR STATUS

Another way to treat your one fan like they're special? Share status and recognition with them.

I've invited several people who follow me across the internet to come out to my theatre in Edmonton to be a "moderator" (essentially a cohost) for my keynotes. To date, I've invited around 60 fans and never received even one no. The stage is fun and exciting; bringing my fans into the action is an easy way for me to show appreciation and overdeliver value.

BRING IN A COSIGNER

Still another way to overdeliver value?

You can always bring others in as "cosigners" on top projects. If you know Rosa is good at graphic design, and you need some input on some content, reach out to her, and then credit her on the project. If Kayla's a rockstar editor, pull her in to proofread your next presentation. Then shine your spotlight on her with recognition in the biggest way possible.

Everyone loves recognition.

BE CONSISTENT,
EVEN THROUGH THE CRASH

Starting any movement can be lonely. I love this line from podcaster Angie Lee:

> Every single successful person that you see doing anything cool started from zero. . . . It's what you give and how consistently you create that rallies an audience.[3]

We all start from zero. Zero followers. Zero likes. Zero support.

From there, it can be painfully slow at first to build up the following you'll need to disrupt.

My wife recently started a podcast, and early on, she felt like quitting, because she didn't find immediate success. I had to remind her that it's in the consistency of execution that followers begin to rally behind you. And then when you hit bumps in the road, it's consistency that will carry you through: Mary Meeker continued to post her report annually despite the internet crash and resulting lack of faith. If you want to build a lasting innovation, you'll need to boldly execute in lonely times. Keep going.

THE NEW WEB

When Kelly released "1,000 True Fans," he was implying that the then-current technology afforded you the possibility of only needing that small number of dedicated fans to create your own powerful following. Likewise with Jin: Her argument was simple—that the technology had evolved even more, and by 2020, you only needed 100 true fans.

Now there's a new tech in town: Web 3.0. With it, I'm arguing, like Jin, that everything has evolved. This technological advancement has so strongly connected one person to one fan, that you can capitalize in a unique way on that singular relationship.

A lot of people have tried to explain Web 3.0. I'm going to make it really simple for you. Let's start in 1996:

In 1996, I was in grade 6 (in America, you'd say "sixth grade"). I was lucky; I naturally understood something about the internet, which made little sense to most of my peers. I figured out how to download small music files onto floppy disks and bring them into school. I showed my friends, and that made me *really cool*, at least for a couple weeks. That was the earliest version of the internet, what technologists now call Web 1.0.

By the early 2000s, the net's new evolution arrived, one built on content creation and engagement. It seemed like every year after that I was adopting a hot new social platform: First, it was AOL IM. Then it was MSN Messenger. Next came Myspace. On its heels, Hi5. Then, in rapid succession, Facebook, Instagram, Snapchat, and TikTok. This was the same period when Kevin Kelly wrote "1,000 True Fans." It was the era of Web 2.0.

But in the midst of all the social media hype, something else was taking shape. People began noticing that tech giants like Google, Apple, and Meta were profiting immensely from our personal data. When you visit a clothing website and click on a pair of jeans, that information is stored, then sold, then reappears in another banner ad. When you tweet a link to your friend's hot new song release, and followers click on that link, the Twitter platform captures that data, then profits. Unless you're an influencer or a tech nerd, all that information has benefited the platform, not you. Apple, Google, Meta, Microsoft, Amazon, and Netflix made billions off this play. And that's when it happened: The individuals whose data was being monetized began wondering, "Where's *my* cut?"

In walked Web 3.0, a new type of technology that, along with other developments such as AI and semantic web functionality, enables each of us to take back our own identity. Instead of a tech giant capturing (and storing) all your data in its own untraceable methods, Web 3.0 stores the info with the individual, in the form of a crypto-enabled "ledger." You own your data, and every time it's accessed, pinged, or tracked, your ledger can notate that information. When utilizing Web 3.0 technology, if you post a link that someone clicks on, your *ledger*, not the platform, will record that click. If you design a video that 100 million people watch, your ledger records who, when, and how.

If your friend Tina *shared* that video, *her* ledger would show who she shared it with. If your video blows up, no longer does Facebook profit from all that traffic. Instead, you, Tina, and all your top fans who shared the video are part of what happened, allowing you to reward every fan like Tina.

Think about a musician, say Sailor Wift, dropping an album. *One* fan, Adam, buys it and then shares it with two friends. They buy it and share it with other friends. And on and on. Each transaction is stored, all the way back in a simple chain of events. Wift can see exactly who her most loyal fans are. Now they are all cocreators of her album, joined at the hip. She could reward each of them, turning her fans into investors with skin in the game. Not just fans, but co-owners.

My point isn't just the technology that underpins Web 3.0. My point is the broader trend. This innovation is forecasting where we're headed: to an era of shared digital identity in which we're all creators, cocreators, and investors in each other's success. One more reason to suggest we've gone from the era of 1,000, to an era of 100, to, finally, the era of 1.

MORE INFO: WEB 3.0

Web 3.0 has multiple other advantages. Eventually Web 3.0 will enable ways to buy "stock" in our favorite musicians, celebrities, or other creators. Since the ledgers record *everything,* we'll be able to receive royalties based on our investment size too. Li Jin and coauthor Katie Parrot said it like this in their essay "The Web3 Renaissance":

> If the pre-internet/web1 era favored publishers, and the web2 era favored the platforms, . . . web3 . . . is all about tilting the scales of power and ownership back toward creators and users.[4]

Web 3.0 provides a system for creators to share their success with their supporters. This new internet will empower individuals more than ever before. It will unlock a community of people around creators who are also invested in their future success.

ONE TO ONE

Bob Goff is a lawyer turned *New York Times* bestselling author and philanthropist. He's wildly popular now—his podcast regularly attracts A-listers like Reese Witherspoon, Mark Wahlberg, and Tim Tebow. He also has his own retreat in California, hosts multiple sold-out workshops and conferences, and is in insanely high demand as a keynote speaker. Here's the interesting thing—he did it by starting with one-to-one connections.

In the back of his first book, *Love Does*—written when Goff was still an entirely unknown construction lawyer—he left his phone number. His *real* cell phone number. Little did he know that he'd sell over a million copies, and basically everyone on earth would soon have his digits. "I still get one hundred calls a day on average. I can't get a thing done. It's terrific," he says.[5]

You'd think that he (or his wife!) would make him change his number or stop giving it out.

On the contrary, Goff has released several more bestselling books, and he puts the same number in the back of all of them.

He picks people up when they need a ride, hops on rides at Walt Disney World with random strangers who call him, and even takes collect calls from people in jail. He won't stop giving out his number, because he knows the power of one-to-one connectivity.

Like Kelly with his "1,000 True Fans" essay, Goff is onto something. No longer does an individual need access to a supply chain, millions of dollars, or complex infrastructure. Instead, you need to convince *one*. Just one person. Built on that, you can create an empire. With the current and coming technology, you can offer one fan something Galileo, Shakespeare, or even Mary Meeker never could—you can offer that fan a piece of your innovation, in a real, solid way.

Remember the unlikely story of David and Goliath, where an underdog, a young sheepherder, beats the big, bad warrior Goliath? We all love a good underdog story. So we often paint ourselves as the small guy fighting "the man." But I want to let you in on a little secret.

The balance of power has shifted to the Davids. Now, more than ever, the Goliaths are terrified of *you*. Individuals are disrupting incumbents.

My prediction isn't that stories like Meeker's are the outliers. Rather in the coming decades, as the Davids realize the Goliaths have lost their power, the Davids will rise up. More and more, individuals will cannibalize entire corporations. We're seeing it in sports, where athletes are becoming more sought-after than their teams. We're seeing it in branding, where people are more likely to buy from a company because of a person. We're seeing it in business, where someone is more likely to buy from a salesperson than a product. One person, one name, can change then game. We've read about it with Ching Shih, felt it with Kutaragi, and watched it happen with Meeker.

In 1801, one pirate claimed her place as the captain of the seas.

In 2010, one woman became Queen of the Net.

What's next for the one reading this?

SECRETS OF THE BOLD ONES

BUILD YOUR OWN MINI-CULT. The three steps to building your own mini-cult, your fan base of exactly one person, are:

Step 1. Declare independence. Too often, employees become overshadowed by their company's own brand. Instead, you must declare independence. You must post, speak, and create in such a way that your own name is attached to the output, even if you don't own the IP.

Step 2. Create something catchy. You've got to create something that is easy to identify. Brand it, make it your own, and make it easy to associate with you and easy to comprehend. Like the hope poster of Obama's 2008 campaign, create an image, a saying, a slogan, something that sticks in people's minds—a ball, if you will, that they can easily catch and toss.

Step 3. Overdeliver to the one fan. Overdeliver value to all your followers. When they comment on your post, reply to each fan individually, no exceptions. Do what takes more effort, and you'll stand out even more.

TAKE ADVANTAGE OF WEB 3.0. In Web 2.0, big tech owned all our data. In the new era of the internet, all of us will possess our individual digital, blockchain-based identities. We own our data now. This makes it easy to trace who has shared what and when, allowing a creator to reward top fans as investors in the creator's success.

CHAPTER 8

HOW TO ENGINEER A HOT STREAK

"Honey, you have to see Hasan's special!"

I joined my wife on the couch to watch the comedy special, *Homecoming King*. Soon I understand exactly why Hasan Minhaj had captivated my wife (and thousands of others). His wit is quick, and he's charming. His political analysis is irreverent yet sophisticated. He incorporates popular culture, and he's uncommonly genius. That's why his Netflix show, *The Patriot Act*, had reimagined the late-night talk show.

The Patriot Act focused largely on somewhat sophisticated political commentary, but with a whole lot of hilarity and a hip technological setup. Think Stephen Colbert meets *Tosh.0*. Minhaj is a South Asian North American. I am too, so I understand the disruptive game he was playing. He was criticizing

American politics as an American but also as a first-generation immigrant. And he was doing it against the backdrop of a political climate that was two years into Donald Trump's presidency.

Within our culture, being a comedian isn't on the table. Or on the wish list. As Minhaj put it, "South Asian parents are highly open with their kids. You can be any kind of doctor you want!"

Minhaj might as well have asked to join the circus as an intern. Sure, his parents may have been proud of him on the opening night of his new, live-audience political comedy show, but all the adventures he had to take to get there weren't exactly smiled upon.

For eight years, he did stand-up at comedy clubs, auditioned for TV pilots, and produced his own content online. Most of this effort came with little return. And then a legitimate opportunity arose when Jon Stewart's *The Daily Show* asked Minhaj to come in for an audition. Stewart himself interviewed and hired Minhaj (it would be the last hire Stewart ever made for the show). That gig allowed Minhaj to continue pursuing his stand-up dreams in the mecca of comedy, New York City. Ironically, though, Minhaj came to an existential realization— he wasn't the best comedian.

Minhaj would watch other comedians own the rooms and absolutely crush it. He performed well but never stirred up the same level of commotion as the greats in his field . . . until he layered in storytelling with his comedy. That's when he found a golden "in."

He took his unique blend of storytelling and comedy to the clubs of New York City. Audiences loved his raw accounts of growing up as an Indian in California, tempered with his comedic hot takes on politics.

With newfound confidence, he created an off-Broadway show. He begged his wife, Beena Patel, to withdraw $27,000 from their joint bank account to rent the Cherry Lane Theater. He called the show *Homecoming King*. He put all his eggs in his storytelling basket and went to work. Within a month's time, the show was starting to sell out.

He took out another $25,000 to shoot a video trailer for *Homecoming King*. He was unabashedly attempting to turn some heads at Netflix to get a nod for one of its coveted specials. He caught their attention, and they filmed his special and slated it for release.

But then things got really interesting.

Remember, Donald Trump was president. White House and press relations were a bit . . . "strained" to say the least. For the first time since the 1970s, the president publicly boycotted the White House Correspondents' Dinner, which generally had been a time when the press and the pres would come together for an evening of comedic solidarity. It was a well-respected tradition, a one-night truce before getting back to the "us versus you" mentality that plagues politics and journalism. But Trump wasn't having it. He wouldn't be going. Then James Corden famously declined *his* invitation to go as well. The upcoming evening quickly became a symbol of the nation's divisions. As Corden's and Trump's responses indicate, many were gun-shy about even showing up. But not Minhaj, who was approached to host the evening. When many weren't putting their hats in for that job, he took advantage of their hesitation. It was risky—one wrong joke, and the president, the media, and/or either half of the country may laugh *at* him, not *with* him. But Minhaj made a bold bet on himself and hosted.

He wasn't just successful. He was a showstopper.

Minhaj later commented that even those who disagreed with his beliefs thought he did an outstanding job as he comedically highlighted that one of America's longstanding values is freedom of the press. The public heralded his performance, and he made headlines globally. The timing couldn't have been more perfect—*Homecoming King* dropped a couple of weeks later, exponentially compounding the spotlight that was already shifting onto him. His star was rising.

And that's when Netflix called (again).

Watching Minhaj's popularity rise high, Netflix wanted to know what else he could do.

Minhaj went back to his wife and asked for another swipe at their life savings. He rented out a recently abandoned state-of-the-art studio. Over one weekend, he and some stage designers and writers built and shot a proof of concept, a sort of pilot episode for what could be a new show. When Minhaj came in to give his pitch to Netlix's co-CEO Ted Sarandos and their team, he played the concept video. Netflix signed him for 32 episodes (a contract they later extended).

Minhaj had successfully jumped through a series of hoops all at once, and for just a moment in time, Netflix, his own talents, popular opinion, and the White House Correspondents' Dinner all aligned perfectly. In one moment, he leaped through a decade of hurdles. Having cleverly said yes to the dinner when others said no, he enjoyed a moment of popularity that may have otherwise cost years to earn.

LIGHTNING STRIKES

If you've ever surfed, you understand perfect timing. Something about catching a wave just right feels like music. The momentum swells and carries you. All the effort, all the trying, all the crashing is suddenly worth it. Studies show something fascinating: Pro surfers spend upward of 95 percent of their time doing everything but surfing—paddling, waiting for the next wave, and watching the horizon. Only 5 percent of their time is spent riding a wave.[1]

If we pretended, for a minute, that pro surfers have a nine-to-five job on the waves, that means, out of their eight-hour workday, they're only spending *24 minutes* actually surfing. Still, they're willing to spend the other seven-plus hours waiting because they know that catching a wave just right is glorious.

In this chapter, we're going to discuss your waves, your moments, your windows of opportunity to strike and strike big. I call these "Lightning Strikes"—when all the hoops align perfectly, and your risk will have outsized returns. Nail this Lightning Strike moment, like Minhaj did, and you'll land a promotion, start a company, or become famous.

How can you prepare for these strikes? And how do you keep them coming? That's what we'll be discussing this chapter:

1. **UNDERSTAND HOT STREAKS.** If a Lightning Strike is a moment in time when everything aligns for maximum impact, a hot streak is getting multiple strike opportunities in a row. Science shows that not only are these possible, but you're likely to experience one in your lifetime, predictably after a period of intense exploration.

2. **PREPARE FOR THE STREAK.** What can we do to prepare ourselves, like Minhaj did, for a hot streak of Lightning Strikes? We can stack our gifts, apply them to unique opportunities, and reflect on what's unique about ourselves. All these activities help us to capitalize on

our moments, the windows of time that are made, seemingly, just for us and our unique abilities.

3. **ENGINEER THE HOT STREAK.** Some say you can't make your streak happen, that it's all left to chance. I disagree. In fact, later in this chapter, I give examples of companies that are doing exactly that—engineering their moments.

UNDERSTAND HOT STREAKS

What's interesting about Minhaj isn't just that he had one big hit. It's that he had a series of back-to-back-to-back *smashes*. He started heating up when he landed his spot as a writer with Stewart; soon after that, he discovered that his true genius is storytelling *combined* with comedy. Next, he had a hit with Netflix, followed by the opportunity to host the White House Correspondents' Dinner, then another opportunity came along with *The Patriot Act*. They all came in rapid succession, in a hot streak.

Hot streaks have been well studied in sports. In athletics, a hot streak typically occurs in a single game after an athlete heats up, and for some reason, that athlete enjoys a few minutes or even hours of insane success: A point guard scores crazy three-pointers in a single basketball game, or a pitcher throws a nine-inning no-hitter. Video games emulate this phenomenon. In many role-playing games or first-person shooters, your character will "charge up" after a few minutes in the game. Then, for a limited amount of time, you get seemingly magical powers, allowing you to defeat opponents with ease.

In life outside of athletics and video games, hot streaks also happen, though usually they occur over the time span of a few years, not within a single evening. An unknown scientific researcher releases one good paper, then another, then another. For a few years, their work is included in every book about the subject, and every media outlet is talking about their discoveries. In music, an artist suddenly releases one big hit. Then their next album wins multiple Grammys, and then, for another couple of years, they do collabs with the hottest producers and artists.

Dashun Wang, a professor of management and organizations at the Kellogg School of Management, has been obsessed with understanding these hot streaks for decades. After studying how these occur, he concluded that people have at least one hot streak in their life. Wang initially suggested that the streaks appear somewhat arbitrarily out of nowhere As he told *Kellogg Insight* in 2021: "Hot streaks seem to happen for most everyone. . . . But it seemed like they come about by 'magic' or just randomly."

While interesting, there's not a lot we can learn from such an analysis. But then—with a little help from the Van Gogh Museum in Amsterdam—Wang started theorizing that maybe, just maybe, there was a bit of order to when those hot streaks appear. He dove back into the research, examining the careers of over 25,000 artists, movie directors, and scientists along with their aggregate millions of pieces of work. After putting all the data in, he teamed up with some hot researchers and sprinkled in some cutting-edge AI analysis. He wanted to see if, beneath the seemingly random occurrence of hot streaks, there *is* a trend. Here's what he came up with:

Hot streaks *are not* random.

He put together a two-pronged framework to encapsulate how streaks occur across every industry for every individual:

PRONG 1—EXPLORATION. For those individuals who experience a hot streak—an extended period of incredible momentum—there's *first* a period of unadulterated exploration, in which they simply discover and "play." The soon-to-be hot streakers first allow themselves to charge up by experimenting in a variety of areas, with varying degrees of success. Maybe they head to the French countryside (like Van Gogh did) and try their hand at different types of art, taking in the ambient sights and sounds. Perhaps a researcher will just let their mind wander, and they tinker around with a variety of seemingly unconnected experiments. This period is a critical precursor to what comes next.

PRONG 2—EXPLOITATION. After exploration, the individuals then prune back their efforts, laser-focusing on what they're most talented at. And then they execute. The result is a series of disproportionate successes that often have more impact on their field and legacy than the rest of their career *combined*.

We can put these prongs together so that we can actually anticipate our hot streaks.

PREPARE FOR THE STREAK

Here's what we want to do: We want to enjoy the period of exploration and prime all the goodness we can out of it so that we prepare for what comes next—exploitation.

The goal during a period of exploration is to find convergences—to identify what you're great at and how that interacts with the marketplace. You need to spend this time discovering, trying, and failing. You should focus on playing more than winning.

By the end (which has no real defined date) you should understand what you're great at and how all of your unique qualities can be pointed at the marketplace.

Your hidden superpowers can arise at the intersection of your role and an intangible: Perhaps you're a financial advisor who can excite people with numbers. Maybe you're a salesperson who listens well, which you find differentiates you among the usually extroverted, fast-talking people in sales. Or perhaps your superpower is buried within your hobbies and has seemingly little to nothing to do with your job. Think of your knowledge of social media, your interest in Bitcoin, your charisma, your self-reflection, your intuition, your design skills, etc.

When you find the intersection of your uniqueness and marketplace demands, you're set up for exploitation—applied science, if you will.

Want a hot streak? Find what makes you hot. Here's how:

STACK YOUR GIFTS

You can combine multiple gifts, just as Minhaj did, in what's called "gift stacking." Simply put together a few areas you're *good* at, so you can create a super-niche in a particular skill set where only you can truly excel.

I've studied the great comedians and others who know how to work a crowd. I've learned from them, and copied them. By combining what I learned with my skill set of the visual arts, I've created a virtual keynote experience that I believe is truly superior. Together, I've created a niche at the convergence of keynote speaking, comedy, and disruption.

Rupi Kaur is another person who's mastered gift stacking. She delivers poetry at live events in addition to being an Instagram artist and a visionary. She's not the best in any *one* of these categories, but she's managed to combine all of them to create a following of millions on Instagram and across the globe.

APPLY UNIQUE GIFTS TO UNIQUE OPPORTUNITIES

Sometimes you can learn a new skill and combine it with a current one when you feel the tide turning. A journalist, traditionally a "writer," may consider the convergence of writing and electronic media and decide to learn web design and computer programming, creating a desired set of skills in storytelling using both written words and website design. Elsewhere, a logo designer may realize that with the uprising in voice, it would be wise to learn how to create "audio logos."

Perhaps you're a lawyer who's also an avid sports card collector, and when NBA Top Shot was thrust into the limelight, you capitalized by delivering legal counsel to those who own and trade NFTs. Or maybe you see a convergence of technologies that appeal directly to your role, your interests, or your experience, and you feel a wave. In any case, when the right wave builds, ride it.

PRACTICE ON SMALL WAVES

Taking advantage of your window in time, jumping straight through when all the swinging hoops align, is a matter of practice, repeated attempts, and continual progress. I don't have an exact answer for when your moment will come, but I can tell you this: You need to be ready when it does. So, I'll say it again: Place small bets. Exercise your innovation muscle and build your tolerance for risk by taking every opportunity you can to bet on yourself.

You can't go all-in all the time; but you can and should bet on yourself in doses. Therefore, it's important for you to continually place small bets on yourself. For example, instead of changing from your insurance job to a videographer role, perhaps you ought to consider asking your boss if you can use your videography skills within your insurance role. Minhaj made incremental bets by experimenting with the storytelling medium and by accepting the invitation to host the White House Correspondents' Dinner. They weren't easy decisions, but they were bets that helped him learn more about himself. You should always be on the lookout for chances to take, for opportunities to place bets on yourself. Remember, you don't have to re-create yourself in a day; you just need to dent the outside, to chip here and there.

Exploration happens *before* exploitation precisely *because* you aren't trained and focused on one area. You must let your mind explore and your skill sets expand. Give yourself the space and time to explore your passions

Then you're ready for what comes next: exploitation.

KEEP A GRATITUDE JOURNAL

While Wang considered exploration to be a specific time period, I think we should always be exploring. And to really capture those moments, so you can look back and say, "Oh, I loved *that* podcasting thing I did," or "Wow! I really enjoyed the convergence of math and graphs," you've got to reflect. So keep a journal.

Specifically, I suggest keeping a "gratitude journal." This helps continually train your mind to always see the *positive* side of everything, even the obstacles. What's interesting is that, upon reflection, my daily "gratitudes" always include serendipity or unexplored opportunities. "I was grateful to run into Jennifer today at the library," or "I was grateful that the flight got delayed so I could learn a new skill on Final Cut Pro."

A gratitude journal helps you capture all the spice of life, meaning that all the exploration you're doing gets documented, helping you remember what makes you "you."

~~WAIT FOR~~ ENGINEER THE HOT STREAK

In 1968, Robert K. Merton, Harriet Zuckerman, and a few others wanted to understand why a small number of scientists and researchers attracted a disproportionate amount of attention from their peers.[2]

They wanted to know why those specific people continued to receive all the press, grant dollars, and prestige in their community, while thousands of other academics were left to split what little remained.

Merton and company discovered that when researchers had a few early successes, they would get cited more often. Then these early citations would parlay them into future successes, because as others cited their work more frequently, they were able to garner more attention and more grant money. With more grant money, they were able to do more research, keeping them in the spotlight and monopolizing necessary resources to keep their research going. Plus, because *others* had cited them, more researchers were disproportionately likely to cite someone who already had plenty of citations. It's the same reason you're likely to go to a restaurant with 100 positive reviews rather than a restaurant with only 10 positive reviews, or why you'll buy an item on Amazon that has 10,000 reviews over one that has only 5 or 10. Once a researcher, a restaurant, or a product has a certain amount of early successes, that particular entity will continue to distance themselves from the pack as others rely on those early votes of confidence.

Merton coined this discovery the "Matthew effect," from which we derive the concept "the rich get richer." Scientists and philosophers have since applied the Matthew effect to nearly every field. Essentially, some people enjoy more fame, popularity, money, or success because they've enjoyed an amount of it previously.

A young soccer player who can dribble, pass, and shoot just one or two notches better than their peers will attract better coaches, who will likely spend a disproportionate amount of time helping them develop their skills. With more skills developed, they'll likely get more playing time. With more playing time, comes more attention from scouts. With more scout attention, they'll have a higher likelihood of landing a scholarship at a good school. With a scholarship at a top university, they'll be exposed to the best practice fields, toughest competitors, and a highly paid coaching staff, all helping them develop into a world-class athlete. The same effect occurs in every field, from science, to music, to innovation.

While I was at Deloitte, there was a policy that ensured every staff member was assigned a mentor, someone who was essentially responsible to look out for a newer employee and advocate for their career success. One of my mentees was Samuel, who wasn't originally on my team; instead, he was blasting away at a large-scale ERP (enterprise resource planning) implementation project. All the while, his real passion was blockchain. He obsessed over it, while the ERP project was sucking the life from him.

Samuel eventually moved onto one of my innovation-related projects, and with that one small step, he came alive. Others in the firm began to network with him, and he took on more and more projects in blockchain. Eventually he left Deloitte and became a strategist at a blockchain-related firm. Then he moved again, becoming the vice president of growth at a blockchain-based application company called Moves. Each success inspired the next. The rich got richer.

But let's take this concept one step further and show how your riches change others' *expectations* of you.

As David Robson pointed out in his book *The Expectation Effect,*[3] scientific evidence suggests that when someone expects X to happen, X is indeed more likely to occur.

So as people witnessed Samuel's success in the blockchain space, they naturally developed an expectation that he would succeed in the future, increasing his odds of success. With every added advantage, his chances of success increased.

Of course, notice that *all* of this is dependent upon an initial success. Note that it's "the *rich* get richer." If you want your efforts to multiply, you've got to start somewhere. In other words, do *something* that will give you this initial success.

While Wang thought you couldn't directly impact when your period of exploitation occurred, I don't buy that. I can show you how some businesses are forcing their own success, creating, at the very least, the appearance of their own hot streaks.

They're using the Matthew Effect and the Expectation Effect to essentially force their own periods of success.

Take the company MSCHF. The company has driven massive results and sales by engineering multiple Lightning Strikes in the form of "drops," specific releases of items on certain days, usually about every two weeks. You sign up via their app, and then on the day of the next drop, the company reveals the piece of clothing you can buy, the standardized test you can take, or the weird video you can watch. Yeah, it's that varied. The company's goal is simple—create anticipation around a big moment in time.

MSCHF is odd, for sure. It's the company behind the infamous Lil NAS X Satan Shoes, in which they put a bit of blood into Nike Shoes, then sold them for about $1,000 apiece (Drop # 43). Before that, on Drop #7, they sold "Jesus Shoes," footwear with 60 ccs of "holy water" from the River Jordan (where Jesus walked on water). Drop #45 was a cookie contest—whoever accepted the most website cookies won 100 pounds of tangible tasty cookies. (User WELP competed and won, with over 140 million website cookies accepted.)

MSCHF has mastered the art of creating its own Lightning Strikes, one after the other. Instead of waiting for "the moment" to jump in, MSCHF engineers it.

So if you want a hot streak, engineer a big moment. Then follow it up again, as often as possible. Here are six steps to make it happen:

1. **SET A DATE AND PUBLICLY COMMIT TO IT.** Whether it's telling your partner, team, friends, or social media following, if you publicly commit to a time or day where you'll make a Lightning Strike, you'll be more likely to commit.

2. **CREATE INTENSITY.** I got this idea from entrepreneur and podcaster Shaan Puri. It's the idea of training your mind to be *intense* about a particular task. By taking a massive action with force, you immediately convince yourself and others that you will do anything to make your ideas happen. So be really, really intense about your drop date. I mean, seriously, be *just a tad* overkill about how awesome this thing is going to be. Tell others; post about it; send a press release to your friends in journalism—do anything you can to drum up buzz and excitement.

3. **BUILD A BIGGER SPOTLIGHT.** This is where you can bring the idea of "cosigning" into the mix. Did someone help you on your project *at all?* Build the momentum by saying, "Hey, this person helped with this, and we're stoked to be releasing it!" One of the reasons MSCHF does so well is that they always co-brand with other exciting entities. Sharing the spotlight really just builds a bigger one.

4. **PROMISE MORE THAN YOU SHOULD.** We often play it safe, by undercommitting and overdelivering. But if you promise more than you should, and still push yourself to overdeliver, you'll create extraordinary momentum for yourself.

5. **VISUALIZE YOUR IMPACT.** Visualize your work having a massive impact on others. If you *know* that what you're doing is a big, good thing for others, then you'll have the motivation to pull it off.

6. **REPEAT.** If you can engineer one Lightning Strike, then you can engineer another, then another.

Here's an example of creating a Lightning Strike for yourself in action.

Let's say that you want to start a podcast about how to create audio logos. You start by inviting a bunch of industry experts in both audio engineering and branding onto your new podcast. You conduct some initial interviews, and then send out the first few episodes to your podcast editor.

Now put a launch date on it. Pick a Friday, a Tuesday, whatever you need, but make it *real*. Commit to it; then blast out a social media post and/or an email, letting everyone know, "Hey, August 1 is *the day!*"

Now sell it—build that intensity like your Lightning Strike moment depended on it. Talk about how awesome your guests are, how amazing your intro music is, whatever you want. Remember to bring in as many cosigners as you can think of—anyone who helped you on this podcast. Tag everyone you can, as publicly as you can, and make it big. Throw the audio engineer, your guests, cohosts, anyone you can think of a huge shout-out. Thank them and praise them often.

Then overpromise. I get it; it's scary to say, "This is gonna kill it!" but honestly, half the battle is in your excitement. If you're excited, and you think it's going to do well, people will too. It's like hosting a party—tell everyone how amazing it's going to be, and people will show up; act like you're unsure if anyone will come, and no one will.

Finally, visualize how much this is going to help others. An audio logo podcast? I mean, come on—that could be *hugely* valuable to brand marketers. Likely they'll learn a ton. Focus on whom you're serving with your drop, and you'll be more excited about bringing them value than you will be nervous about your acceptance.

Now, for the final step:

The hot streak. Take that new podcast you've created, hype it up, get everyone involved, overpromise and overdeliver, and then do it *again*. Keep striking; keep building. Create your own momentum, and make that hot streak appear, whether it wants to or not.

YOU'VE GOT TO HIT "PUBLISH"

For some people, sharing themselves with the world is scary. I get it.

I have an attorney friend whom we'll call Raj. He's a fantastic lawyer, but his superstrength is *storytelling*. None of the modern storytelling greats, such as Dave Chappelle, Kevin Hart, or even Barack Obama can beat Raj.

You're probably thinking, *If he's so great, why haven't I heard of him?*

That's exactly my point: He hasn't shared himself.

If you're like Raj, hitting "publish" on your content, finally releasing your mobile app, or raising your hand and asking your boss a question can be a bit scary, particularly for my introverted friends. But you've got to conquer that fear, because you're going to need attention at some point. So, get all the work done, then, *hit* "publish."

DON'T BE A HODAD

Your big moments won't always scream, "Hey, now's the time to jump in." In fact, sometimes the seemingly worst possible times are the very instances you should jump in.

In 2020, the world stood arrested as a pandemic shook humanity. I had given a few keynotes already that year, but soon I watched as the ecosystem for keynote speakers was entirely disrupted. What would I do next?

Other speakers turned to a poorly produced virtual avenue, with a spotty digital platform and a talking head appearing over a grainy laptop camera. That was the best most speakers came up with—plenty just canceled altogether.

I saw the moment as something that could be huge for me. I could just feel it: Video, digital, and charisma are all in my DNA. No one else was seeing the opportunity to create an enhanced virtual keynote experience, but I was seeing the confluence of the world's needs and my natural abilities.

So, I asked my team, "Can we create the greatest livestream experience ever witnessed?" Was it a big question? Sure. But I wanted to elevate the game.

My team didn't disappoint. They said "yes, and," bringing their own ideas in. Soon we rented the 700-person Myer Horowitz Theatre. We bought Hollywood-quality digital cameras, and we tripled down on our video production game. My team and I carefully plotted how to capture my charisma on stage and transport it across a digital platform.

After a couple of virtual keynotes that my team rocked, other conferences heard that I was available and prepared to go fully digital. They called and booked me. More and more weekends started filling up. By the end of 2020, I'd spoken at more conferences than I had in 2019. And in 2021, I had my best speaking year ever.

I can give you strategies and pro tips all day about engineering your own hot streaks, but in the end, it's up to you.

Surfers have a name for those who hang out on the beach all day and have all the trappings of a surfer—they have the suits, the music, and maybe even the cool hair, but they never actually jump in. They're called "hodads." And you *never* want a surfer to call you that.

After consulting with dozens of CEOs and frontline workers, large firms and small companies, tech unicorns and stodgy enterprises, I've concluded that the only behavior that truly distinguishes between disruptors and the disrupted is this: Some jump in, and some don't.

So here's your invitation:

Jump in.

Start preparing for your streak as if it's inevitable. Grab all your skill sets, and point them at the market in the most ferocious way you can. Disrupt the conversation with your excitement. Make people pay attention.

And when it's all said and done, take the leap.

SECRETS OF THE BOLD ONES

CREATE YOUR OWN LIGHTNING STRIKES. These are unique moments in time where your efforts create an outsized impact. At any other moment, the same action may never garner the same attention as a Lightning Strike opportunity affords you. When you see these windows of time open up, you must take advantage.

UNDERSTAND HOT STREAKS. Multiple Lightning Strike moments in a run create a hot streak—a period when you can seemingly do no wrong. Research shows that most people will experience at least one hot streak in their professional career:

you'll get promoted repeatedly and rapidly, your ideas will gain extreme favor with your colleagues and the marketplace, and even media can come looking for you.

EXPLORE AND EXPLOIT. While difficult to predict, research shows that your hot streak is likely to be precipitated by a period of extreme *exploration*. During this time, you should try your hand at a variety of skills, many of which you may never fully develop. But somewhere in the mix, your superpowers become more obvious and more refined. Then, you start to focus on your unique gifts and talents, pointing them at the marketplace in way that makes sense for the current climate. By focusing your efforts on these superpowers, the marketplace rewards you, and you may enjoy a period of *exploitation*.

ENGINEER YOUR OWN HOT STREAK. You can wait for your window of opportunity for exploitation, or better yet, you can create your own moments by engineering Lightning Strikes, back to back. Here's how:

Set a date and publicly commit to it.

Create intensity.

Get others involved.

Promise more than you should.

Visualize your impact.

(Repeat.)

CHAPTER 9

DISRUPT A CULTURE; LEAVE A LEGACY

Egypt, 1479 BC. Thutmose II passed away. His son, Thutmose III, will be pharaoh one day, but not yet. He wasn't old enough to rule. So, as was tradition, until her stepson was of age, Hatshepsut, the half sister and wife of the late Thutmose II, stepped in to help rule, as a regent. This was a common tradition, the appointment of someone older and wiser who would act as a temporary ruler for a short time until the true ruler was capable of claiming his or her rightful place.

And that's where Hatshepsut's rule should have ended—as a small dash, maybe simply an asterisk, in the annals of Egyptian history—the wife, half sister, and stepmother who managed to keep the throne warm between her husband's and her stepson's powerful reigns. But it turns out, she had other ideas . . .

From the moment she was declared regent, Hatshepsut found herself caught in an odd gap between great religious power and nothingness. She'd been acting as the God's Wife of Amun for years. It had been her job since she was a young girl to "awaken" the god Amun every morning in his holy temple.

After becoming regent, she was on the verge of being too old to arouse Amun, so her religious duties would pass to her daughter. Then when her stepson came of age, she'd lose her regency.

But during her regency, she did something perhaps no other woman in history had done—she claimed the throne, fully. Not as *regent*, but as *pharaoh*.[1]

There were multiple problems with her ascension, besides her sex. For one thing, her stepson had already been named king, and this was a well-known fact across Egypt. Second, the kingship officially passed through the gods, typically from father to son.

She was far too clever to assume she could just brush these points to the side as trivialities. Instead, she used her knowledge of the deep truths (the gods) to reveal that they, along with her father (previously a pharaoh), had *chosen* her to be king. Clever indeed—who can argue with the gods?

By some accounts, she propagated an occultic narrative, the sort that whetted the religious appetites of the Egyptians—writing on some hieroglyphics that, apparently, her mother had been impregnated with the seed of the gods, so Hatshepsut was literally conceived by the gods. On official sculptures, hieroglyphics, and engravings, she predated her kingship to the day her husband passed (which was about seven years before she declared herself pharaoh), matching it in time to that of her stepson's kingship. In other words, she erased time itself, and backdated her own rule to prove her legitimacy, as if to say, "I was never regent, but always king."

To handle the problem of her sex, she even bent the rules of Egyptian language (there was no real word for "queen," for instance). Eventually, she even adopted a masculine image in many of the drawings and sculptures—not to deceive, but to show strength and legitimacy.

It's hotly debated, but some consider Hatshepsut the first female pharaoh. What's not debated? That she was one of the most powerful pharaohs, male or female, in Egyptian history. She was instrumental in developing many of the greatest Egyptian monuments, in particular, the great temple complex Deir el-Bahri ("the monastery of the North"). She led her country through a relatively peaceful period, and she expanded trade with East Africa and the Mediterranean, importing all sorts of things—among them, ebony, gold, wood, myrrh, and exotic animals.

In the end, she was a political genius and a master of religious affairs, and she can be found on every scholar's list of "the greatest pharaohs." But you probably haven't heard much about her—ironically because that's just how powerful she really was.

After she passed, someone (likely Thutmose III) removed her likeness from many of the writings and histories, most notably from the list of kings.

She was one of the greatest ~~female~~ pharaohs who ever ruled.

CULTURAL DISRUPTORS

Today society is obsessed over a singular type of disruption: the disruption of business via technology.

Whenever someone says "innovation" or "disruption," we immediately think of a young solopreneur using technology to run a business from her home. While lounging in her pajamas and eating avocado toast, the disruptor upends a monolithic incumbent all from the convenience of her MacBook and home-made latte.

But if we pull back the curtains on history, disruption isn't just about business, and it certainly doesn't only come through technology.

Disruption is about an upheaval of the status quo, wherever it exists:

- Shakespeare disrupted the *arts* and *society* by bringing the elites and the masses together through stories.
- Henry Ford disrupted the *process* of industrialization by utilizing the assembly line.
- Mahatma Gandhi disrupted *colonialism* through his peaceful methods.

Hatshepsut did something deeper than oust a company. She disrupted a culture.

Cultural disruption sits at the peak of everything we've discussed—it's the ultimate play, describing how one individual can implant themselves so deep into the hearts and minds of a community, that their next move, however audacious, changes how we view life itself, social norms, and even political balances of power.

These types of disruptors will outlast the technologies they invent, or the powers they fight. They even outlast their own time on earth, because once they leave, the patterns of our minds have altered so much that the rest of us continue the work they started. Disruptors like that don't truly die when they take their last breath; instead, they live on in the haunting of our own decisions and activities.

In this chapter, we're going to explore what it takes to disrupt a civilization, to change the very air that's breathed, and to change the way life is lived. How do you do this?

1. **CREATE A VINCE CARTER EFFECT.** If you want to disrupt a *culture*, you've got to do something so powerful that it outlasts your own activity. When Vince Carter won the 2000 NBA Slam Dunk Contest, he inspired a generation of Canadian basketball players.

2. **USE THE POWER OF STORIES.** *Sleeping Beauty, Batman, Thor.* These all inspire, because they're engaging, shareable, and magical. If you want to inspire a generation, get really, really good at telling stories.

3. **INVITE OTHERS IN.** To disrupt a culture, you'll need others. You'll need to spread your ideas from person to person, and you'll need to surround yourself with other innovators, to draft off the power of those around you.

4. **FOLLOW THE MAYA PRINCIPLE.** Hatshepsut was ambitious but careful. She set her sights on the moon, but then she took it slowly, finding the most disruptive, yet tolerable, idea. She was willing to push the envelope, but not beyond what those around her would allow. Likewise, we've got to find a way to think big, but not *too* big.

While in 2022, most are studying the Bold Ones who are challenging technologies, I believe the real game we should all be playing is the one Hatshepsut started thousands of years ago:

How can we disrupt the universe?

THE VINCE CARTER EFFECT

I'm taken with how Vince Carter utterly overtook the 2000 NBA Slam Dunk Contest.

At the time, as Carter pulled off moves the world had never seen before, every dunk was like watching a futuristic basketball game. The most iconic move came when Toronto Raptors' player Tracy McGrady passed the ball to Carter, who put it through his legs and finished with a thunderous one-handed slam.

I've watched the entire evening on replay dozens of times, but I actually missed watching it live—I was a teenager at the time, and I was out with my family. So I had whipped out the VHS player to videotape the episode, old school.

When we came back home, we kept hitting rewind, as time stood still while Carter laughed in the face of gravity.

While Carter disrupted the dunk competition, his resulting legacy disrupted a generation: Youngsters from around Canada (where Carter was born) began leaping toward the basket with a fierceness no coach could have inspired. Carter spirit descended on Canada, from Halifax to Victoria, as kids began dunking, spinning, and flying toward the hoop.

Canada's a country of only 30 million people, but after Carter's performance, we produced a disproportionate amount of impressive NBA players such as Jamal Murray, Andrew Wiggins, RJ Barrett, and Shai Gilgeous-Alexander.[2]

In the 2021–2022 season, there was a total of twenty-five Canadian players in the NBA, with four more added in the 2022 draft, two of whom were drafted in the top ten.[3] By then, Canada's national team bragged that it had the most NBA players on it, second only to the United States itself.

That's the Vince Carter Effect: the creation of dozens of basketball godchildren.

By the time he retired, Carter had never won an NBA championship, nor did he become MVP. Instead, he alley-ooped for the next generation of Canadian b-ballers.

How can we all create our own Vince Carter effect, where our ideas don't just start with us, but outlast our own activities?

For starters, we've got to do something visual.

I'm all for words, but if you want to implant your idea into someone's mind, you've got to do something everyone can see. Scientists have conducted thousands of hours of research on the power of visual cues. If you check out the scientific literature, you'll find dozens of papers that include terms like "retinal ganglion cell" that discuss the power of human visual recognition. Basically, all the science supports what journalists have known for years, that a picture truly is worth a thousand words.[4]

Recently, a colleague we'll call "Randall" was trying to get ahold of a Fortune 500 company, one of the top general merchandisers in America. He'd cold-emailed them several times to pitch his idea. Of course, he got no response. So he started slow-dripping *pictures* of his product to them. He got responses from two directors

That's the power of visuals. I'm all for excellent copywriting, but you can stop people in their tracks with a mind-bending visual appeal.

Hatshepsut incarnated herself, her ideas, and her reign by creating various visuals including dozens of hieroglyphics, tombs, temples, the Sphinx of Hatshepsut, and at least four obelisks. She commissioned the largest obelisk in the world ("the unfinished obelisk") and had others placed at the temple of Karnak.

One of them is 3,500 years old and still standing.

Take your disruptive idea, whatever it is, and wrap it in a visual. Here are some ways you can do that:

- **GET THEM ON-SITE.** Is there a way you can connect your disruptive idea to something people can visit, not just read about? There's a reason you remember all your field trips from school, and very little of what the field trip was about. Can you bring "them" (whomever you're trying to convince) to the factory floor, to the headquarter building, or to wherever the magic happens? I can describe the *Mona Lisa* all day, but there's nothing like standing a few feet away from it at the Louvre. If you can't get them in the door, stream it or make a video of it and send it to them.

- **BORROW THE VISUAL TEAM.** If you aren't the visual aficionado you wish you were, swap some work with a coworker or a colleague. Trust me; graphic designers and videographers are usually stoked that someone recognizes their chops, so pet their ego, and bring them in. It's a lot easier to take your coworker out for coffee than it is to learn Adobe InDesign.

- **THINK *YOUTUBE*, NOT *WORD*.** Look, I get it: In some industries you need charts and lots of math to convince head honchos. Or so people say. When I first joined Deloitte, all my comrades were pitching our clients with lots of numbers in black and white that said, "My idea is awesome, and here's why, with revenue and profits to back it up." They'd compile a genius plan; then "paint" it with a bunch of lingo and drop it inside a 30-page notebook. After printing it off they'd hand the colorless, word-heavy document to their clients.

Not my team—when we pitched, we often made video presentations of our ideas. Our advice wasn't necessarily better, but all our clients thought it was. They were so enthralled with our presentations, we got yesses when my colleagues heard no, simply because we used video when they went traditional. A visual representation of what you're doing is always worth the extra effort.

USE THE POWER OF STORIES

Skyler Irvine, CEO of RenzlerMedia, once said this on a call, "The story is always the most valuable." I totally agree. In fact, I say it like this:

**The most powerful person in the room
is always the storyteller.**

From comic book superheroes to Cinderella, from the origins of the universe to the *Origin of Species*, from Batman to *Band of Brothers*, stories become the iconic ideas that inspire, unite, and rally humanity.

In *The Woman Who Would Be King,* author Kara Cooney lays out exactly how Hatshepsut was able to overcome her womanhood to transcend to a place few, if any, women before her had dared to go.

Hatshepsut tapped into the power of story.

Consider her origin narrative about how the god Amun had visited her mother to conceive Hatshepsut. In the hieroglyphics, we also find supernatural tales of how the gods supposedly chose Hatshepsut. She didn't need to bother with reality, because the legends themselves were so engaging, she'd captured the imaginations of her constituents.

The greatest stories don't just provide the needed inspiration, but offer a touchstone, a point from which people can add to create their *own* story inside your universe.

Consider the most successful game creators, comic book writers, and authors: They all create macro cosmoses so large, that there's room for not only their own stories, but the stories of others.

- Dungeons & Dragons (D&D) is an entire world of gameplay that encourages players to each build their own characters. D&D created the platform; others leap from it.
- Comic book creators design such detailed and expansive characters, places, and powers, that dozens of writers, artists, actors, and directors can keep adding, expanding, and re-creating for decades.
- Writers such as J. K. Rowling, J. R. R. Tolkien, and George Lucas develop such captivating stories, that there's a whole genre of work called "fan fiction" created by others.

When well executed, these stories are often so extensive we call them "universes," and you can find this type of ever-expanding universe in business as well.

The company Salesforce, whose flagship product is a customer resource management tool, has created its own universe: Its software platform is so ubiquitous that numerous third-party businesses offer Salesforce add-ons. Annually, Salesforce hosts its Dreamforce conference where hundreds of companies and over 170,000 people often gather to connect . . . It's like

Comicon but for a sales software platform.[5] Salesforce has created a universe so large, it's a breeding ground for others.

If we want a lasting legacy in this world, we must create a story that captures others' imaginations, and simultaneously inspires them to create their own stories inside of ours.

If you want to know how to create a story, read a book on Greek gods and goddesses, or check out the *Star Wars* series, and apply what you're learning to the tale you're trying to tell. Particularly, you'll need these elements.

SHARE A BAD-ASS ORIGIN STORY

Your storytelling starts with why you're doing this, how we all got here, or why this is important *to you*. Clare Potter was a fashion designer who started in the 1920s. She has a remarkable backstory: She was a horse rider, and she was tired of having nothing to wear. That was her origin story, which became the springboard from which she created some of the world's first female riding outfits. Later she was instrumental in creating the women's two-piece bathing suit, the precursor of the bikini.[6]

What's your origin story? What ticked you off, why did you start this, and what was the moment that this idea became critical for you?

NAME THE VILLAIN

In May 2022, Crumbl cookies cofounder Jason McGowan released a Twitter thread he titled "The Billion-Dollar Decision," telling his followers that in 2022, Crumbl would do $1 billion in sales. The Twitter thread was an iconic rags-to-riches story, detailing how the cofounders could barely afford the $300-per-month rent originally, and nearly closed up shop; and then, voilà, a few years later, they were the epitome of the American dream.

Everything was going fine until, Crumbl believed, two of its competitors committed trademark infringement. So Crumbl sued the two competitors. One of the companies being sued, Dirty Dough, rapidly created a villain out of Crumbl, seizing on its big corporate bad guy status and turning the public against Crumbl. Dirty Dough founder Bennett Maxwell told *Utah Business*:

> **Apparently, this billion-dollar company, Crumbl, is threatened by a startup with only a couple of locations to make a federal case out of rainbow sprinkles and rectangular boxes.**[7]

Then, in a LinkedIn post, Maxwell added this:

> **Watch out Grandma, you better throw away those sprinkles or you will be Crumbl's next victim.**

Oh, and then he released a picture of potential billboards that said things like, "Our cookies don't crumble with competition."

Maxwell successfully painted Crumbl as the large, billion-dollar corporation trying to copyright grandma's cookies and stifle competition.

The public backlash was almost instant.

Dirty Dough had successfully created a corporate villain, named the villain publicly, and rallied everyone who likes cookies, competition, or grandma.

I was on LinkedIn at the time, typically known for its professional behavior, and the comments and the tags directed at McGowan and the rest of the Crumbl team were pretty vicious.

You don't need to attack a real company to name a villain (although that was pretty effective). You need to name the villain you're after: If you're innovating to overcome inefficiency, call out inefficiency. If you've created a process that will save thousands of wasted hours a year, call out waste. If your idea will stop pollution, call out pollution. Name that villain, and rally the followers.

MAKE IT MAGICAL

In *Inception,* Leonardo DiCaprio's character, Cobb, builds a team whose mission is to plant an idea deep into someone else's mind. Others believe it's impossible, but Cobb knows it can be done, *if* you travel deep enough into the person's imagination.

If you want to penetrate someone's mind, you've got to infiltrate that person's imagination. When Carter dunked one-handed after passing the ball *between his legs,* it was hard to miss. Every time I remember that dunk, it's a little more fantastic than what actually happened. My imagination creates an echo chamber and combines it with the game of telephone. When I share that story, it gets exaggerated, just a tad:

"Did you see Carter's one-handed dunk?!"

"I know! I swear he *flew.*"

With your story, start with something a bit *magical.* Without Carter's gravity-defying jumps, no one would have imagined that he could nearly fly. Initially, he planted the thought. The best stories always have something a little magical, something just out of the ordinary about them, to spice everything up.

Take gum commercials, for example. They often show attractive, young people chewing gum, then meeting the person of their dreams. Apparently, the gum's a magic potion. Sure, we don't really believe that the stick from Trident will help us find true love, but I mean, it can't hurt to try, right? The commercial plants the idea; our minds do the rest.

Connect the product you're creating, the service you're providing, the content you're delivering, or the process you're pioneering to something one notch out of the ordinary. Then go ahead and plant the idea that the blog you're writing about marketing and sales coming together could totally change the way corporate culture runs. Be a little edgy the next time you're advocating for your team to branch out into a new line of business: "Think of how many zeros in revenue this could create." Go for it. Make it a bit magical.

KEEP IT SIMPLE

Simplify; simplify; simplify. Far too often we make the stories too difficult to understand and digest for our audience. We can't name the villain, the solution, or the problem in layperson's terms.

Simplicity is difficult to achieve, but easy to share.
Complexity is easy to achieve, but hard to share.

If you want to tickle people's ears, make the pitch smooth, seamless, and simple: "No restaurant in Canada is serving this kind of food. We'll be the first." Or "Project management in construction is wildly inefficient. This new process could save millions." Find the hook, drill it home, and, to repeat, keep it simple.

INVITE OTHERS IN

To basketball fans born before the 1980s, the name "Michael Jordan" is synonymous with "the greatest basketball player of all time." But when my nephews, born after 2000, think of Michael Jordan, they look down at their feet, at their Air Jordans. To them, Michael Jordan is the shoe guy. If I asked them about him, I'm sure they'd have some vague recollection that he played basketball. They'd probably even note that "a lot of people think he was really good." But in the end, it's the shoes that matter to my nephews.

MJ transfigured from the GOAT of the court to the god of footwear. His kicks are so legendary, people are still wearing them, whether or not they've even seen him play. He built something more viral than his "product," basketball.

Cultural disruption isn't easy. We've talked a lot about building a fan base thus far, but there are two more concepts to keep in mind:

1. BUILD SOMETHING MORE VIRAL THAN YOUR PRODUCT

Just as MJ did, try to build something that outlives a fascinating product or service. Remember the "sexy angle" we talked about in Chapter 7, with the drones? That went viral. What can you release that can outshine and outlast your core offering?

Hatshepsut built some of the worlds' greatest obelisks, and people still visit them to this day. Her laws, decrees, and political influence may no longer prevail, but she built something so lasting, we can't forget her.

2. SURROUND YOURSELF WITH OTHER INNOVATORS

Secondly, if you want to inspire cultural disruption, you'll need help from those around you. I like to tell my team, "Never show up to a battle without an army."

In his book *Wanting*, author Luke Burgis talks about mimetic desire, a concept originally developed by French philosopher and polymath René Girard.

Burgis and Girard both posit that our innermost desires often aren't ours at all, but that we're simply mimicking the desires of others. We want the Ferrari because Joe wants it. We want the scholarship because Angela has it. I've watched as my son picks up a previously discarded truck, lying on the floor near a group of other children. Suddenly that truck is the object of every child's desire.

If you apply this to how to disrupt a culture, you'll find a huge upside: Once you start innovating, you'll ignite the innovation desires of others. They see how the marketplace rewarded you, how the industry recognized you, and they want the same. This is the kind of innovation fire you need to start, be a part of, and champion, if you want to truly disrupt a culture.

In the best way possible, innovation is a contagious, dangerous game. And like any infectious organism, it spreads in *proximity*.

It's one thing to read about Walt Disney, but I'm sure it was quite another to be in the room with him while he talked about animating *Snow White and the Seven Dwarfs*. I bet the room became a crucible of innovative ideas.

That's one reason Silicon Valley pumps out so many awe-inspiring technologies—the valley is a hub of innovative tech, and it just keeps attracting more innovators, like a magnet.

You can also look at Russell Simmons's TV show, *Def Comedy Jam*. When he put together black comedians from across the country to challenge and excite each other, a who's who of the world's greatest comedians emerged: Martin Lawrence, Chris Tucker, Chris Rock, Dave Chappelle. I could go on with iconic names for paragraphs.

If you put our mimetic desires in a room with other contagious innovators, the results are contagious, as we each challenge and inspire the best in each other.

FOLLOW THE MAYA PRINCIPLE

Elisha Otis first introduced passenger-safe elevators in the 1850s. At that time, elevators were run by elevator operators, often called "porters." The porters were in charge of operating the elevators for passengers, ensuring that an elevator stopped correctly on each floor. Without a trained and strong porter who could operate the original heavy levers, the elevator could miss the floor you were attempting to stop on, or it could move before someone was fully aboard. The porters were vital for safety and efficiency.

By the 1900s, automatic elevators began to hit the market—these required no elevator operator to safely maneuver. But there was a problem—people wouldn't use the automatic elevators. In many cases, they simply refused. They were so accustomed to having a porter, they couldn't imagine the elevator just magically "stopping." What if someone's foot gets stuck? What if the door closes early? How will we open the door when we get to our floor? So for almost half a century, elevators continued to operate with porters, for no reason except that people weren't ready for automatic elevators.

But then someone came up with a hack, a trick, to get around people's hesitancy. An automatic speaker with a recorded system was installed in each elevator. The system instructed passengers how to operate the elevator themselves. As Steve Henn put it on *NPR*'s *Morning Edition* in 2015:

> **There was a soothing voice piped out of the speakers when you walked inside. "This is an automatic elevator. Please press the button for the floor you desire."[8]**

Pause for a second to consider how entirely unnecessary this system was. Did the passengers really not know which button to push for their correct floor? I'm fairly certain every person going to level three knew that the button with the big 3 on it was most likely the best option. The problem was fear. People needed something, an in-between step, to help bridge the gap between porter-operated elevators and automatic elevators. So, wisely, a simple hack was introduced. A soothing voice that gave instructions.

If you're going to do something big, sometimes it's necessary to mask that innovation with the most disruptive, but still acceptable, idea people can handle today. The idea is actually backed by science, and it's called the "MAYA principle."

"MAYA" stands for "most advanced, yet acceptable." It means that when you're introducing a disruptive idea, technology, or process, you want to offer the most outlandish version possible, *but* it still has to be palatable to your audience.

When Hatshepsut rose to the throne, she did so as a co-heir; she tied her female kingship to the male kingship of her stepson. Was she more powerful than he was? Absolutely. Was she a greater pharaoh than he was? Undoubtedly. However, if she had simply thrown off the old ways and spat in the face of tradition entirely, she likely would never have been successful. She was daring, but not crazy. She pushed the boundaries, but not past the breaking point. She used the MAYA principle. As author Cooney said:

> **As she had done all her life, she moved deliberately, step by step, claiming new titles and names when she thought the time was right, never pushing it beyond what those around her could tolerate.**[9]

There are myriad ways to bring a brighter future into the present in a seemingly safe way. For you, the Bold One, these safety mechanisms may seem unnecessary—and you're probably right. But they help others take a step into disruption, and they give you a jump-start in getting your idea off the ground.

People of the old guard may have a problem accepting an edgy idea—they just can't wrap their minds around it. Why not help them by adding in a traditional feature? For example:

- **CERTIFICATIONS.** Third-party recognition does a lot for people of tradition. Let's say you want to open a new channel partner income stream. Your boss is hesitant. Why not get a channel partnership certification, just to make your boss feel safer? There are numerous places online you can go to get certified in just about anything. Does a piece of paper make you a master at something? No, but others don't need to know that.
- **LEGAL STAMPS OF APPROVAL.** Especially in large corporations, you can run ideas by the people in your legal department to get their sign-off. In the same way a certification makes people feel confident in your abilities, when a lawyer says, "Go ahead," others around you feel safe to proceed.

- **KEEPING JUST ENOUGH OF THE OLD PROCESS.**
  Sometimes you can keep just enough tradition to
  make everyone feel comfortable while introducing a
  virtually new idea. For instance, if you want to use a
  new AI-driven hiring process, perhaps you can instill
  confidence with your HR department by keeping some
  of the old questions from the manual interviews. Later,
  once you've proved that your AI process is actually
  better at reducing discrimination and finding the best
  applicants, you could drop the old questions.
- **SAFETY BUTTONS.** There is another thing that the
  automatic elevator disruptors did to make everyone
  feel safer. They added in "the biggest calming device
  ever invented, a big red button that said, stop."[10] These
  buttons helped give people a way out. In *Never Split the
  Difference,* author and former FBI hostage negotiator
  Chris Voss shows that giving others the power to say
  no is exactly what you need to do to get them to say yes.
  It's the counterintuitive argument that we so often miss.
  When people feel in control, they think clearly and
  they're more likely to engage. When you trap them into
  saying yes, they're simply looking for a way out. So offer
  a "safety button" to your team, your boss, or whomever
  you're trying to convince. A back-out-anytime-you-
  want clause, a money-back guarantee, or a "no pressure,
  here's the offer" pitch will actually perform far better
  than the traditional assumptive close, especially when
  dealing with disruption.

The illusion of control gives people the sense of security they
need to try something that they perceive as dangerous.

THE RESURRECTION

Joseph Campbell's seminal work, *The Hero's Journey*, recounts the steps that every hero in every great story takes. One of them, about three-fourths through his journey, is this—resurrection. Once the hero comes back to life, he changes the game. He may have had victories—or in our case, minor disruptions—before his death, but *after* he dies and comes back to life, he's endowed with new, supernatural powers.

Hatshepsut died around 1458 BC. She was a disruptor while she lived, but she'd have to resurrect herself to become a goddess.

And she did.

Hatshepsut was perhaps Egypt's first full-fledged female pharaoh, but she certainly *isn't* Egypt's most well-known female ruler. That title belongs to Cleopatra, who came about 1,500 years after Hatshepsut.

But here's the thing, Cleopatra isn't *Cleopatra* without Hatshepsut. Who knows if Cleopatra would ever have made it to her throne without the rise of her predecessor? Hatshepsut disrupted a culture, an entire civilization. She'd captured hearts and minds, implanting herself into the very imagination of her civilization. Perhaps unknowingly, her life was a stepping-stone for the most famous female ruler in Egyptian history. If we take it a bit further, perhaps Hatshepsut's pursuit of the throne paved the way for *all* female leaders since then. She might just be *the* Bold One who created such a universe in which there could be a female head of state, CEO, or founder. "If Hatshepsut did it, so can I" may have been Cleopatra's thoughts. And how many people has Cleopatra inspired?

It took 1,500 years between Hatshepsut and Cleopatra, but in 2022, there will be *26* female heads of state across the globe.

There absolutely could (and should) be more, but perhaps there wouldn't be as many without Hatshepsut as inspiration.

When you sacrifice yourself on the altar of disruption, your legacy isn't contained to your last move; instead, it continually reverberates in *their* next move.

Bold Ones don't wait for permission, for anyone to invite them. They take their place at the table, or they build their own. They find a way in, a way around. Along the way, they inspire others; they infect the marketplace with new methods, new systems, and new products. They discover, create, fail, repeat.

The world doesn't make room for Bold Ones and their ideas; Bold Ones *reshape* the world as needed. When you first picked this book up, you already had an idea, a thought, a crazy desire. Something keeps you up at night—in the deep throes of the internet, in the chat rooms. You're interested; you're looking; you're searching. Inside your cubicle, you know how to improve the processes. You see inefficiency that can be removed. You believe in the reshaping of an industry.

It's time to jump, to make a bold move, one that requires taking a chance. Put some skin in the game, and make a little noise. Likely, when you do, you'll find others who've been thinking the same things all along. When you do ruffle some feathers—and you will—just remember what Oscar Wilde said:

**An idea that is not dangerous is unworthy
of being called an idea at all.**

SECRETS OF THE BOLD ONES

CREATE A VINCE CARTER EFFECT. Vince Carter never won an NBA championship, but, after *seeing* his electrifying dunks, an entire generation of Canadian basketball players rose up. If you want to disrupt an entire culture, you've got to show them what it *could* be like. Going through the eyes always works better than going through the mind. Bring people on-site, use power-packed visuals, and utilize videos to convey your disruptive vision. Show, don't tell.

UP YOUR STORYTELLING GAME. The most powerful person in the room is the storyteller. The better your stories, the more followers you can inspire. Use these specific elements to tell captivating stories: a "why" behind the mission, a villain, a bit of magic, and simplicity. Add those in, and you'll capture imagination.

BUILD SOMETHING MORE VIRAL THAN YOUR PRODUCT. You're going to need others onboard. The best way to create something shareable is to think well outside of your product or service. Michael Jordan created shoes, and they've outlived his prominence as a basketball player. What's something creative you can make that others will share?

FOLLOW THE MAYA PRINCIPLE. You want to push people into disruption, but never past what they can tolerate. Often, your ideas may be so wild, others can't quite understand how they would work. So, use certifications, legal stamps of approval, or safety buttons, or mix in just enough of a traditional process to convince others.

CONCLUSION

In 1893, Samuel Zemurray, a teenage Russian Jewish immigrant, stumbled across a yellowish gold mine in the United States. More accurately, he stumbled across a yellowish *fruit*. If you want to get truly exact, he stumbled across a yellowish fruit with two dots that was "ripe."

You probably think of "ripe" as meaning "good to eat." You'd be correct. However, "ripe" in the 1890s also meant that it was only days from being spoiled. Bananas—not native to the United States—that arrived on the docks with two or more freckles would be thrown into the ripe pile to be destroyed.

Zemurray had an idea—if he could buy those ripe bananas on the cheap, hop on a train, and sell them quickly before they truly spoiled, he could turn a profit. He negotiated a deal, bought the would-be-trash pile of bananas, then hopped on a train. He sent a wire ahead to all the grocers in the various towns up the train line to meet him at the train stations, and he'd sell them his soon-to-be-spoiled but still excellent-tasting bananas straight from the boxcar.

His plan worked, and he turned a profit. So naturally he did it again. Then again—buying ripes and turning them into treasures. What began as one train car of nearly spoiled bananas started an empire. Soon he'd spread across the country, and out of it, into the continent where the bananas actually grew, South America.

By 1910, he was pushing further into Honduras. There, to keep profits high and taxes low, he'd need certain concessions from the local government. He'd risen from the status of immigrant to businessman. By 1910, Zemurray's reputation had already earned him the nickname "Sam the Banana Man."

A man of few words and decisive action, he generally got his way. But Honduras wasn't playing ball. So Sam the Banana Man did the most brash, bold thing you could do:

He decided to overthrow the government.

In 1911, he bootstrapped a rebellion from the streets of New Orleans, scrounging up mercenary fighters and meeting with a former ousted president of Honduras, Manuel Bonilla. Then he loaded up a warship he bought from the US Navy, and he headed south to overthrow the government that wouldn't appease him.

One day, he was an immigrant selling bananas out of boxcars. A few decades later, he was putting rifles on his boat bound for another continent, financing a coup d'état in a foreign nation.

Zemurray, just as he always did, got his way. He overthrew the government.

Later he toyed with the Guatemalan government until *its* leader was also overthrown.

Oh, and he was fundamental to the creation of the state of Israel too. When the Jews were fighting the Arabs in the 1940s after World War II, most Western countries, such as the United States and Great Britain, had a don't-get-involved policy, and shipping guns to support either side was illegal. But Zemurray had an armada of ships (indeed his ships were seized by the US government during World War II to help with the war effort) and plenty of money, and, of course, he was Jewish. He sent guns and money to the Jewish fighters in the Middle East. Then, when the United Nations voted *against* approving the newly created State of Israel, Zemurray got on the phone with his South American contacts, who were the swing votes in the United Nations. After a few phone calls—and potentially some money sliding hands—there was a revote. A few key players in South America had miraculously changed their votes, and the country of Israel was born.

Zemurray was a world disruptor. The very makeup of political boundaries today might not be the same if it weren't for him.

When Zemurray bought that first bunch of ripe bananas in 1893, he purchased them from the very company he'd need to fight later, United Fruit.[1]

United Fruit and Zemurray went head-to-head for decades, fighting wars in the political arena, and very nearly fighting their own wars with their own guns on banana lands in South America. But by 1929, it was clear that both could not fight the external forces while also fighting other banana kingdoms. So in 1929, United Fruit and Zemurray joined forces. He sold his company, and United Fruit gave him stock. He gave up his land rights, and United Fruit made him its de facto chief executive officer.

Consider the unlikely turn of events: One day, a young teenager was buying a company's trash to scrounge a few pennies.

Three decades later, he was president of that very company, the largest fruit company in America.

If you've ever had a banana in the Western hemisphere, likely you've tasted Sam the Banana Man's legacy. United Fruit underwent complex bankruptcies and mergers in the latter half of the 1900s, until it became a brand you know of with the trademark blue and yellow logo: The brand today is called Chiquita.

———

Zemurray was certainly a controversial figure. He certainly wasn't Mother Teresa, and his dealings in South America were, in the best light, capitalistic to the extreme. But here's what I love about Sam the Banana Man: The man who virtually single-handedly overthrew the Honduran government didn't use new technology, he didn't revolutionize weaponry, and he didn't define an era with his aircraft. He disrupted governments, effectively, with a soft yellow fruit.

He saw a problem, innovated, and then innovated again. He kept following this path of disruption, a path that made its way into the pages of history, through the countries of Latin America, and into our grocery stores. He wasn't a chemist, and he didn't have the engineering mind of an Elon Musk. He simply had an idea, and he went for it. He sold some bananas, then sold some more. He just didn't see impossibility the way others did. They'd say it was impossible, and he'd shrug as if he didn't quite understand the meaning of that word. And maybe he didn't; after all, he was an immigrant.

The point is, Zemurray, like all Bold Ones, saw what no one else saw, and to him, it wasn't impossible. It was just the next step on his path.

You can't underestimate the power of your own innovative ideas. You don't have to leave your country, your industry, or even your company. Kutaragi stayed with Sony. Simmons still writes. Ching Shih was (almost) always a pirate. Meeker still releases the "Internet Trends" report. Hatshepsut was always Egyptian. You don't even need to be in technology. Cardi B is a rapper. Hasan is a storyteller.

You can innovate at your desk today. The next time you feel that itch, that burning deep down to speak up in the meeting, to send the email and ask the question, "But *why* do we do it this way?" just ask. Speak up. Be curious. Wonder. Ask why, and keep asking.

The moment you see your ripe banana opportunity, take it. You never know where it will lead.

NOTES

CHAPTER 1

1. https://www.gamesradar.com/playstation-25th-anniversary-how
   -sony-created-the-console-that-redefined-the-game-industry/;
   Garfinkle, Joel A. *Getting Ahead: Three Steps to Take Your Career to
   the Next Level.* John Wiley & Sons, 2011.
2. https://venturebeat.com/2018/06/23/the-story-behind-nintendos
   -betrayal-of-sony-and-how-it-created-its-fiercest-rival/.
3. https://www.digitaltrends.com/gaming/bestselling-consoles-of-all
   -time/.
4. https://www.amazon.com/Ken-Kutaragi-PlayStation-Developer
   -Innovators/dp/0737738626.
5. The origin of this quote is disputed; thought leader and business
   author Peter Drucker is often given credit for it.
6. The premier is to a Canadian province what a governor is to a US
   state.
7. On the Billboard Hot 100.
8. From *The Matrix*.

CHAPTER 2

1. https://www.youtube.com/watch?v=23orFHrxdps&
2. A triple-double occurs when an NBA player achieves three double-digit statistics in three of these main categories: assists, blocks, points, rebounds, and steals.
3. Greatest of all time.

CHAPTER 3

1. https://www.domusweb.it/en/design/2021/09/21/the-percentage -of-creativity.html.

CHAPTER 4

1. Duncombe, Laura Sook. *Pirate Women: The Princesses, Prostitutes, and Privateers Who Ruled the Seven Seas.* Chicago Review Press, 2017.
2. There were other pirates in other parts of the world who also created pirate federations and codelike regulations for their respective territories.
3. https://cdapress.com/news/2022/feb/20/history-corner-chinas -pirate-queen/.
4. Italics mine.
5. Tracking down this quote's origins has been difficult. Most agree that Hubbard said it exactly like this, or something very similar. Many sources suggest that science fiction historian Sam Moskowitz was the first to document Hubbard's utterance of this exact quote in a 1994 affidavit that Moskowitz wrote. That affidavit, again, has been difficult to find. In the supposed affidavit, Moskowitz supposedly claimed that Hubbard said this at a 1948 meeting hosted by the Eastern Science Fiction Association.
6. https://www.apa.org/monitor/julaug02/eminent.
7. https://www.adidas-group.com/media/filer_public/e9/73/e973acf3 -f889-43e5-b3c0-bc870d53b964/2015_gb_en.pdf.
8. https://www.refinery29.com/en-us/2022/02/10873570/rihanna -savage-x-fenty-interview.

CHAPTER 5

1. Academics disagree on this quote's origin.
2. In this book, I refer to Jamsetji Tata by his first name to distinguish him from the rest of his family.
3. An innovative YouTube-based educational institution. Check it out!
4. https://www.businessinsider.com/amazon-buys-twitch-2014-8.

5. https://earthweb.com/twitch-statistics/#:~:text=Twitch%20has%20 30%20million%20daily,had%2055%20million%20active%20users.
6. https://www.linkedin.com/pulse/contrarian-marketing-manifesto -peter-weinberg/.
7. https://www.history.com/topics/middle-east/yom-kippur-war#:~: text=On%20October%206%2C%201973%2C%20hoping,day%20 in%20the%20Jewish%20calendar.
8. Kuperwasser, Yosef. *Lessons from Israel's Intelligence Reforms*. Saban Center for Middle East Policy at the Brookings Institution, 2007.
9. Most of Israel's policies are fairly secretive, but some analysts have suggested that not only is the concept of the tenth man alive and well in Israel, but the country may have an entire unit dedicated to Devil's Advocate thinking.
10. Barnea, Avner. "Devil's Advocate: A Methodology to Improve Competitive Intelligence." *Competitive Intelligence* 22, no. 3 (Summer 2018).
11. Peterson, Jordan B. *12 Rules for Life: An Antidote to Chaos*. Penguin, United Kingdom, 2018.
12. https://www.aboutamazon.com/news/company-news/2018-letter -to-shareholders.

CHAPTER 6

1. Monitor Deloitte is a sister company that specializes in strategic consulting.

CHAPTER 7

1. https://kk.org/thetechnium/1000-true-fans/.
2. https://li-jin.co/2020/02/19/100-true-fans/.
3. https://www.forbes.com/sites/stephanieburns/2020/09/18/from-a -100-microphone-to-millions-of-downloads-top-tips-for-building -a-raving-podcast-audience/.
4. https://every.mirror.xyz/y_WLA-Tk3VF5uPqHi-glDLVVfHxLU bjXakRI7SMISas.
5. Goff, Bob. *Dream Big*. Thomas Nelson. Kindle Edition, p. 59.

CHAPTER 8

1. https://journals.lww.com/nsca-jscr/fulltext/2014/10000/the_effect_ of_wave_conditions_and_surfer_ability.31.aspx.
2. Merton, Robert K. "The Matthew Effect in Science: The Reward and Communication Systems of Science Are Considered." *Science* 159, no. 3810 (1968): 56–63.

3. Researchers have identified a number of phenomena that could fall under the expectation effect. The Pygmalion effect, placebo effect, and halo effect are a few popular examples.

CHAPTER 9

1. Some scholars say she was the first true, full-powered pharaoh; other scholars say that Nitocris or Sobekneferu, who came before her, was the true first.
2. https://www.complex.com/sports/best-canadian-nba-players-right -now/dillon-brooks.
3. https://www.sportingnews.com/ca/nba/news/full-list-canadian -players-in-nba-2021-22-season/ml0ooa2v6ua31ar4qpmig53m1.
4. https://www.ncbi.nlm.nih.gov/pmc/articles/PMC4574956/#:~ :text=All%20primates%2C%20including%20humans%2C%20 are%20highly%20visual%20creatures.&text=We%20rely%20 heavily%20on%20visual,the%20formation%20of%20social%20 hierarchies.
5. https://www.sfexaminer.com/archives/dreamforce-returns-with -hundreds-on-hand-down-from-170-000-in-the-past/article_ effb9906-f98d-595a-abc4-a029127fc00b.html.
6. https://www.nytimes.com/1999/01/11/nyregion/clare-potter-who -set-trends-in-women-s-clothes-dies-at-95.html.
7. https://www.utahbusiness.com/utah-cookie-wars-dirty-dough -responds-to-crumbls-lawsuit/#:~:text=%E2%80%9CApparently %2C%20this%20billion%2Ddollar,boxes%2C%E2%80%9D%20 says%20Bennett%20Maxwell.
8. https://www.npr.org/2015/07/31/427990392/remembering-when -driverless-elevators-drew-skepticism.
9. Cooney, Kara. *The Woman Who Would Be King: Hatshepsut's Rise to Power in Ancient Egypt.* Crown Publishing Group, New York, 2015.
10. https://www.npr.org/2015/07/31/427990392/remembering-when -driverless-elevators-drew-skepticism.

CONCLUSION

1. Some may point out that, technically, the company he purchased the first ripes from was Boston Fruit Company, which merged with others later to *become* United Fruit.

SOURCES

CHAPTER 1

On Kutaragi

https://venturebeat.com/2018/06/23/the-story-behind-nintendos
-betrayal-of-sony-and-how-it-created-its-fiercest-rival/.

From Aubrey to Drake

https://wqhs.upenn.edu/started-from-the-bottom-now-we-here-a
-detailed-look-at-drakes-early-career-and-rise-to-fame/.

https://www.insider.com/drake-life-career-timeline-2018-10#
aubrey-drake-graham-was-born-on-october-24-1986-1.

https://www.gq.com/story/rapper-drake-in-america-july-2013.

https://www.koimoi.com/hollywood-news/drake-creates-history
-breaks-michael-jackson-beatles-record-on-billboard-hot-100/.

https://www.eonline.com/news/1169618/every-record-breaking
-moment-in-drakes-career.

https://www.gq.com/story/rapper-drake-in-america-july-2013.

CHAPTER 2

On Putin

https://www.businessinsider.com/berlin-wall-today-compared-to
-before-it-fell-photos-2018-2?r=US&IR=T.

The Russell Westbrook Trap

https://www.sportingnews.com/ca/nba/news/nba-all-time-leaders
-most-career-regular-season-triple-double-russell-westbrook/
5ikkunwbz0el1az4567yvr5t7.

From 100 to 0

https://www.youtube.com/watch?v=_J4ZUJ38t0c.

CHAPTER 3

3% Rule

https://news.harvard.edu/gazette/story/2017/11/harvard-welcomes
-virgil-abloh-for-gsd-lecture/.

CHAPTER 4

On Ching Shih

Cooney, K. *The Woman Who Would Be King: Hatshepsut's Rise to Power in Ancient Egypt.* Crown Publishing Group, New York, 2015.

Duncombe, Laura Sook. *Pirate Women: The Princesses, Prostitutes, and Privateers Who Ruled the Seven Seas.* Chicago Review Press, Chicago, 2017.

Teller, Tom. *Ching Shih, Pirate of the China Seas: From Prostitute to Pillager Queen.* Kindle edition, 2013.

On Victoria's Secret/Savage Fenty

https://www.usatoday.com/story/money/shopping/2021/02/24/
victoria-secret-store-closures-2021-bath-body-works-opening/
6806159002/.

CHAPTER 5

On Jamsetji

https://www.google.com/books/edition/Jamsetji_Tata/siHIDAAA
QBAJ?hl=en&gbpv=1&printsec=frontcover.

Lala, Russi M. *The Creation of Wealth: The Tatas from the 19th to the 21st Century*, Penguin Books, India, 2004.

Sharma, Yagya. *Jamsetji Tata*. Amar Chitra Katha, 2007. https://www.amazon.com/gp/product/B06VT26PHL/ref=x_gr_w_bb_glide_sout?ie=UTF8&tag=x_gr_w_bb_glide_sout-20&linkCode=as2&camp=1789&creative=9325&creativeASIN=B06VT26PHL&SubscriptionId=1MGPYB6YW3HWK55XCGG2.

https://www.theguardian.com/books/2022/jan/06/the-expectation-effect-by-david-robson-review-mind-changing-science.

https://reference.jrank.org/psychology/Halo_Effect.html.

https://www.financialexpress.com/archive/in-the-shade-of-the-taj-mahal/230600/.

https://lifestyle.livemint.com/news/talking-point/jamsetji-tata-the-make-in-india-pioneer-111646894682199.html.

https://www.tata.com/newsroom/through-the-mill.

CHAPTER 6

On Michele Romanow

https://www.youtube.com/watch?v=pQuyUNwbP9U.

https://www.youtube.com/watch?v=HCgcpuYBHKw.

https://medium.com/authority-magazine/how-michele-romanow-of-dragons-den-succeeds-and-thrives-as-both-a-celebrity-and-an-entrepreneur-eab900aad5c3.

https://www.womenofinfluence.ca/2021/10/07/meet-michele-romanow-co-founder-president-of-clearco/.

https://piemediagroup.com/digest-blog/michele-romanow/.

https://fortune.com/2019/07/31/clearbanc-dragons-den-facebook-instagram-ads/.

https://www.theglobeandmail.com/report-on-business/small-business/sb-growth/how-we-acquired-six-companies-in-a-year/article13107242/.

On Starbucks

https://finance.yahoo.com/news/35-years-milan-apos-espresso-111918402.html.

CHAPTER 7

On Mary Meeker

https://archive.fortune.com/magazines/fortune/fortune_archive/2001/05/14/302981/index.htm.

https://www.nytimes.com/interactive/2022/03/18/technology/web3-definition-internet.html.

https://www.singlegrain.com/web3/web-3-0/.

https://www.youtube.com/channel/UC8jscPMHNVYhZ0Zg3b9NeTA.

https://www.amazon.com/1000-True-Fans-Kellys-Simple-ebook/dp/B01N9P9O4G.

https://www.nytimes.com/2018/09/14/technology/mary-meeker-kleiner-perkins.html.

https://www.barrons.com/articles/SB914023727750233000?mod=article_signInButton.

https://www.inc.com/larry-kim/10-inspiring-facts-about-venture-capitalist-mary-meeker.html#:~:text=In%201998%2C%20Barron's%20Magazine%2C%20a,a%20multi%2Dbillion%20dollar%20company.

https://www.wired.com/2012/09/mf-mary-meeker/.

https://business.time.com/2012/07/20/the-ten-most-influential-women-in-technology/slide/marissa-mayer/.

https://www.institutionalinvestor.com/article/b1f48yckxt48v6/Kleiner-Perkins-Spin-Out-Raises-1-25-Billion-in-Less-Than-Four-Months.

On Barack Obama

https://www.npr.org/2011/05/03/135840068/the-singular-woman-who-raised-barack-obama.

On Li Jin

https://li-jin.co/2020/02/19/100-true-fans/.

https://future.com/passion-economy/.

CHAPTER 8

On Hot Streaks

https://insight.kellogg.northwestern.edu/article/artists-scientists-career-hot-streak.

https://www.theatlantic.com/ideas/archive/2021/11/hot-streaks-in-your-career-dont-happen-by-accident/620514/.

Liu, Lu, Yang Wang, Roberta Sinatra, C. Lee Giles, Chaoming Song, and Dashun Wang. "Hot Streaks in Artistic, Cultural, and Scientific Careers." *Nature* 559, no. 7714 (2018): 396–399.

https://insight.kellogg.northwestern.edu/article/career-hot-streaks.

https://www.nature.com/articles/s41586-018-0315-8.

CHAPTER 9

On Hatshepsut

https://www.worldhistory.org/article/118/queen-hatshepsut-daughter-of-amun-pharaoh-of-egypt/.

https://www.bbc.co.uk/history/ancient/egyptians/hatshepsut_01.shtml#:~:text=The%20female%20king%20vanished%20from,king%20vanished%20from%20Egyptian%20history.

https://www.historyhit.com/famous-ancient-egyptian-pharaohs/.

https://www.thenationalnews.com/mena/egypt/2022/04/10/ancient-obelisk-re-erected-in-original-location-at-luxors-karnak-temple/#:~:text=One%20of%20two%20obelisks%20bearing%20the%20name%20of%20ancient%20Egyptian,Karnak%20on%20April%209%2C%202022.

https://www.history.com/topics/ancient-history/hatshepsut#:~:text=%2Dday%20Eritrea).-,Hatshepsut's%20Death%20and%20Legacy,hills%20behind%20Deir%20el%2DBahri.

https://www.history.com/topics/ancient-history/hatshepsut.

https://www.youtube.com/watch?v=8bYRy_wZEJI.

https://www.worldhistory.org/hatshepsut/.

https://www.bbc.co.uk/sounds/play/b04n62jx.

https://books.google.com/books?hl=en&lr=&id=pvhNq307q9gC&oi=fnd&pg=PR12&dq=hatshepsut+became+pharaoh&ots

=cW0A8cWsMm&sig=g5V_5iaJsBBIrEwwqoCywFXk1as#v=
onepage&q=hatshepsut%20became%20pharaoh&f=false.

https://papersowl.com/examples/hatshepsut-and-cleopatra/.

https://www.unwomen.org/en/what-we-do/leadership-and-political
-participation/facts-and-figures.

On Crumbl

https://www.businessinsider.com/crumbl-files-federal-lawsuit
-against-cookie-competitors-2022-7.

https://www.utahbusiness.com/utah-cookie-wars-dirty-dough
-responds-to-crumbls-lawsuit/.

https://www.azcentral.com/story/entertainment/dining/2022/07/22/
crumbl-sues-dirty-dough-tempe-arizona/10128512002/.

https://www.sltrib.com/artsliving/2022/07/22/crumbl-ceo
-doubles-down-utah/.

https://twitter.com/jasonmcgowan/status/1529488695404859393?l
ang=en.

https://www.utahbusiness.com/utah-cookie-wars-dirty-dough
-responds-to-crumbls-lawsuit/#:~:text=%E2%80%9CApparently%
2C%20this%20billion%2Ddollar,boxes%2C%E2%80%9D%20
says%20Bennett%20Maxwell.

https://www.linkedin.com/in/bennett-maxwell-703717126/recent
-activity/shares/.

Other

https://www.ncbi.nlm.nih.gov/pmc/articles/PMC4574956/#:~:text=
All%20primates%2C%20including%20humans%2C%20are%20
highly%20visual%20creatures.&text=We%20rely%20heavily%20
on%20visual,the%20formation%20of%20social%20hierarchies.

https://www.sfexaminer.com/archives/dreamforce-returns-with
-hundreds-on-hand-down-from-170-000-in-the-past/article_
effb9906-f98d-595a-abc4-a029127fc00b.html.

https://www.sportingnews.com/ca/nba/news/full-list-canadian
-players-in-nba-2021-22-season/ml0ooa2v6ua31ar4qpmig53m1.

https://www.complex.com/sports/best-canadian-nba-players-right
-now/dillon-brooks.

https://www.sciencedirect.com/science/article/pii/S004269891100
2458.

CONCLUSION

On Sam "Sam the Banana Man" Zemurray
http://www.unitedfruit.org/zemurray.htm.

https://curioushistorian.com/the-banana-king-the-powerful
-businessman-who-helped-rescue-jews-and-launch-political-coups.

http://content.time.com/time/subscriber/article/0,33009,744983,00
.html.

ACKNOWLEDGMENTS

This book needed an entire army of Bold Ones to help get it done. First and foremost, I have to thank my wife, Deepa. She is my biggest cheerleader and supporter. Whether it was at dinner, a walk, or a long-car ride, she has heard me stress-test every concept of this book in some form or fashion throughout the years. Deepa has known me since high school. Every single one of my career achievements is because of her encouragement and support.

Can everyone stand up? I want to give a standing ovation to Paul Fair. Paul is one of the greatest writers and storytellers that I've had the pleasure of working with. We spent months together over Zoom during the pandemic, fleshing out these ideas. He would take my half-baked stories, brain dumps, and hundreds of pages of YouTube transcriptions and turn them into magic. He would push me and extract every piece of information from my mind, and then he would do it again. I would never have been able to do this book without Paul's immense talent and dedication to *The Bold Ones*.

I am grateful to my literary agent, Connor Eck. I can't say enough great things about Connor. He's helped me navigate every single part of the publishing process. He has been such an incredible partner and advocate. Most importantly, since we first connected in 2019, he's believed so strongly in me. Connor is the primary reason this book has come to fruition.

Many people ask me why I chose McGraw Hill as a publisher. I give them a simple answer: Cheryl Segura. It was the best decision I made for this book. She made *The Bold Ones* a hundred times better than it was after its first draft. She pushed to make the book more tactical, and we moved mountains to make it happen. Cheryl was an absolute joy to work with.

I would not be here without my speaking agency, Speakers' Spotlight. The founders, Martin and Farah Perelmuter, and the entire team have helped me carry this message of disruption everywhere. We've conquered the entire world together, and we haven't even started!

I can't tell you how much it means when I get a message from someone telling me how my work has impacted them. To every single person that has read this book, watched a video, sent me a DM on LinkedIn, commented on a TikTok, yelled at me across the street—thank you!

And, finally, to my kids, Dhyan and Maya. You inspire me every single day. I get to see the world again through your eyes.

To me, you are the *boldest* ones. Don't forget it.

Love you all. Thank you.

INDEX

ABOUT THE AUTHOR

SHAWN KANUNGO is a globally recognized innovation strategist and keynote
speaker. He advises organizations and
executives on disruptive trends. He
previously spent 12 years at Deloitte
working closely with leaders on strategy and innovation. In 2021, Forbes
called him the "Best Virtual Keynote
Speaker I've Ever Seen." He was named
"Top 40 Under 40" by *Edify* magazine.
Kanungo's stories on innovation have garnered millions of views
across LinkedIn, TikTok, and Facebook.